MONDAY MORALITY

Monday Morality

Right and Wrong in Daily Life

Edward Wakin

PAULIST PRESS
New York/Ramsey

Designed by Ellen Foos

Library of Congress
Catalog Card Number: 80-80871

ISBN: 0-8091-2317-7

Published by Paulist Press
Editorial Office: 1865 Broadway, New York, N.Y. 10023
Business Office: 545 Island Road, Ramsey, N.J. 07446

Printed and bound in the
United States of America

Contents

1

Drawing the Line

"I don't like these questions because I've struggled with them in 'real life' and find the choices difficult."

Everyday morality is hardly noticeable. It's a private affair. No fanfare, no placards, no rallies, no public acts of civil disobedience, not even a letter to the editor. It involves "difficult" choices in "real life," choices that don't always fit into neat slots of right and wrong.

The choices vary—depending on the situation, on the circumstances, on the facts, on the interpretation of facts, on the individual.

Would you lie to save someone's feelings? To avoid a traffic ticket?

Exaggerate education and experience in order to get a job?

Take supplies home from your job?

Tell the whole truth when selling your used car?

What exceptions would you make in your everyday moral code for a friend? For a member of your family?

Such issues are not cosmic, not about detente, nuclear fallout or pollutants in the ionosphere. Nor do they involve deregulation or the price of gold, juvenile justice or national health insurance, cost-of-living or minimum wage. These issues are typically handled at a distance with words, a check in the mail, a signature on a petition, a trip to the ballot box—all necessary, commendable, morally uplifting, and done at arm's length.

Everyday morality does not keep its distance. It hangs around the house, goes with us to store, school, and work, and tags along on vacation. Day in, day out, each of us weaves an individual life of right or wrong. As the French essayist Montaigne aptly observed, "every action reveals us"; we can judge a horse "not only by seeing it ridden at a gallop, but also by its walk, and even by the sight of it resting in its stable."

When political rhetoric evaporates, when Congressional hearings fade from the screen, when Sunday sermons are extinguished with the altar candles, concerned Christians are left with moral decisions on how they live each day with what it brings. Life stories are woven out of details, incidents, routines, an everydayness that eventually makes a life, a mixture of the conscious and unconscious, the examined and unexamined. For the churchgoer, after worshiping Sunday there is meaningful (or meaningless) Monday. After Sunday sermon, there is Monday morality.

A labyrinthine trip through everyday morality with answers given by hundreds of individual Catholics and Protestants around the country uncovers the *what's*, *how's*, and *why's* of the choices made. When a number of moral theologians were asked as expert guides to add their views, they raised similar questions and produced similar variations—all starting with their common foundation in the twofold Commandment of Love (in its secular version the Golden Rule):

> "You shall love the Lord your God with your whole heart, with your whole soul, and with your mind. This is the greatest and first commandment. The second is like it: You shall love your neighbor as yourself. On these two commandments the whole law is based, and the prophets as well."

While the Golden Rule or its Christian version was not at issue, application to specifics was another matter among both lay Christians and theologians. As Father Timothy O'Connell, chairman of the Christian Life Department at St. Mary of the Lake Seminary in Illinois, pointed out, Christian morality is based on "commitment to the good," but "it can be very difficult to find the good and we need all the help we can get." The problem is further complicated by the difference between *ought to* and *must* in judging moral behavior. The influential theologian, Father Charles E. Curran of Catholic University, emphasized the difference between what he thinks is wrong and what he can—as moral theologian—"oblige people to do."

Professor Roger Shinn of Union Theological Seminary, one of American Protestantism's most influential moral theologians, referred to Augustine who tended to "sum up ethics as love and do as you please, but even he gave some guidelines." Dr. Shinn described himself as sympathetic to the view that "basically the loving person can be trusted to do right more than the non-loving person who has a book of guidelines." In noting that Catholicism generally has built morality on prescriptions, he gave his view of guidelines: "Given our frail human nature, guidelines would be helpful and I would draw them sooner rather than later."

In a broad sense, lay responses differed on where to draw the line in making moral choices. A Lutheran teacher of Bible studies compared the process to teaching a child that a red light means STOP. Yet there are exceptions where red means stop, look, and then go ahead (as when right turns are permissible at red lights). This can be confusing out on the street just as in the real world where being moral does not always require or even mean stopping at *Thou Shalt Not* signs.

Listening in on others makes the listener aware of his or her own moral process. It's a way of comparing notes and of taking a second look at what someone will and will not do. For some, WRONG, WRONG, WRONG was enough of an answer for one situation after another. For others, morality left room for conscientious exceptions, with some drawing the line sooner than others.

Rule-directed Christians resisted exceptions and showed concern about "taking the easy way out." They were uneasy about what would happen "if everyone did it" and they were not going to do something "just because everyone's doing it." Theirs tended to be a black-and-white world.

Situation-directed Christians were more comfortable with exceptions and were reluctant to invoke rules just for rules' sake. They looked toward other people, toward circumstances and consequences. They tended to see more gray in their world.

3

A theologian of situation ethics might divide the two types of answers into a rule-bound legalistic approach and a principle-bound situational approach. But that is too neat a division for the variety of answers given to any single question and to the variations in answers from any single person. People don't live as students in a school of moral theology. They apply common sense, a certain amount of moral knowledge, personal experiences, and individual attitudes.

In the process, they do a creditable job of reaching moral conclusions that parallel the more formal conclusions of moral theologians. In fact, the laity consistently echoed the answers of the moral theologians and vice versa. I was impressed by the fact that practically every lay answer had an equivalent among the professionals. Even on abortion among Catholics.

The cabdriver whom theologian Joseph Fletcher described as the "hero" of his book on situation ethics has allies everywhere. The cabdriver was explaining why he was going to abandon his life-long Democratic commitment and split his ballot to vote Republican for the first time: "There are times when a man has to push his principles aside and do the right thing."*

In reflecting on differences in moral responses, theologian Margaret Farley spoke from her unique vantage point as a tenured professor at Yale Divinity School who is also woman, Catholic, and nun. As preamble, Dr. Farley cited the four "base points" used by theologian James Gustafson in a widely-cited article that grapples with the confusion over situation ethics.** Four key areas of consideration are involved in a moral decision: (1) the situation or context as analyzed by the individual; (2) the moral rules and principles which are important to the individual; (3) the moral decision-maker and his or her needs, capabilities, perceptions; (4) the fundamental theological beliefs (or fundamental world view) of that decision-maker.

Any decision informed by consideration of these four "base" points may be "objective" in a certain sense, but it is also bound to depend in an important way on who the decision-maker is. Differ-

* Joseph Fletcher, *Situation Ethics* (Philadelphia: Westminster Press, 1966), p. 13.
** "Context Versus Principle: A Misplaced Debate in Christian Ethics:" by James Gustafson, *Harvard Theological Review*, vol. 58 (1965), pp. 171–202.

ent folks make different decisions: "People look at different things when they analyze a situation. It depends on their world view. We filter certain things *in* and certain things *out*."

"To a certain extent," Father Curran noted, "decision is king and a person makes a decision according to his or her own integrity. I can see there is going to be a pluralism of possible actions in many issues. Even within the Catholic Church, I am a great exponent of the fact that we are going to have much more pluralism than we ever had in the past."

That pluralism casts a wide net that encompasses both Catholics and Protestants. In recent years, as Catholic moral theologians disagreed among themselves, Catholic and Protestant moral theologians have readily agreed on many issues. In noting the closeness, theologian John Milhaven of Brown University, author of *Toward A New Catholic Morality*, sums up current Catholic-Protestant differences on morality as "slight." "In fact," Father Curran observes, "on the level of Catholic ethics as lived in the Catholic community I do not see any distinctive aspects."

Catholic morality can no longer be characterized as a clear-cut set of *do's* and *don'ts* authoritatively handed down by the Catholic Church and automatically accepted by the laity. The "manual approach" belongs to the past, a time when Catholic seminarians studied manuals of moral theology that tried to cover every conceivable situation. This prepared the priest in the confessional to provide unequivocal judgment, sentencing, and forgiveness of whatever thoughts, words, and deeds were whispered in semi-darkness on a Saturday afternoon.

When critics complained that pre-Vatican II Catholics confused the letter with the spirit of the law, morality seemed to be confessional clear, particularly with regard to sex. Moral mandates left no doubts, and if there were any, Catholics looked to the Church for a clear, unequivocal answer that made up their minds. And the moral issue was closed.

Something dramatic happened to this view of Catholic morality on the way back from Vatican II. Individual Catholics were called upon to carry their own burden of moral reckoning, instead of letting priest and Church carry it for them. U.S. bishops expressed this emphatically in a 1966 pastoral letter: "No one is free to evade his

5

personal responsibility by leaving it entirely to others to make moral judgments."

Catholics were challenged to work out their moral blueprints. As explained by Father Frank McNulty, professor of moral theology at Darlington Seminary in New Jersey, "the focus is more on a good person trying to live a good life and taking responsibility for that life himself or herself." As never before, American Catholics answer for themselves when faced with moral choices, rather than depend on someone else to make the choices.

For Catholics, declarations of independence became public, emphatic, and controversial after Pope Paul VI's 1969 *Humanae Vitae* encyclical banning "artificial" birth control. Extensive surveys by the National Opinion Research Center at the University of Chicago showed that almost four-fifths of Catholic clergy and laity disagreed with the encyclical. In taking issue with the encyclical, laity, clergy, and moral theologians took on the hierarchy. The fallout from their independence still affects bedroom, rectory, and chancery.

Other surveys show that Catholics and Protestants are even close together in their views of such traditionally divisive items as birth control and divorce. One study of Catholic and Protestant moral styles led to the observation that "there seems to be little difference between American Catholics and American Protestants in moral judgments, although in some cases Catholics tend to be more 'flexible,' or 'less strict,' than Protestants (but also less flexible and more strict than Jews).* When *McCall's* magazine reported on the responses of 60,000 readers (May 1978 issue) to a religious survey, the "most significant differences of moral opinion" among Christians was not between Catholics and Protestants (except on abortion). It was between those Christians who consider themselves "born again" and those who do not.

Looking on from his Protestant background, theologian Shinn noted that he could readily recognize differences in the way Protestant and Catholic theologians argue to their conclusions. (Catholics would use more quotations from the Vatican and from Catholic

---

* Andrew M. Greeley, *The American Catholic* (New York: Basic Books, 1977), p. 247.

documents.) But as to conclusions, "it would be hard to find a difference that I'd recognize readily." Both Catholic and Protestant moral theology include what he called "a spectrum" from fundamentalist to situationist, with both groups "much closer together than ever." It's even possible to talk of a convergence.

Fundamentally, Christ is the common denominator of Christian morality; what benefits the human condition the common concern. "Nonbelievers may have a strong motivation coming from commitment to a human value system," moral theologian Gregory Kenny, a Claretian priest, said. "But Christians add witness to their beliefs, demonstrating belief in Christ as the model of what humanity should be. Christians have the mission of showing the possibilities of humankind as they were worked out in Christ."

As C. S. Lewis observed in discussing Christianity, morality makes you sensitive:

> When a man is getting better, he understands more and more clearly the evil that is still left in him. When a man is getting worse, he understands his own badness less and less. A moderately bad man knows he is not very good: a thoroughly bad man thinks he is all right. This is common sense, really. You understand sleep when you are awake, not while you are sleeping.... You can understand the nature of drunkenness when you are sober, not when you are drunk. Good people know about both good and evil: bad people do not know about either.*

So this is an account of *getting better* when Christians face the difficult choices of Monday morality. It is designed for those concerned about the question, "If you were accused of being a Christian, would they find enough to convict you?"

---

* C. S. Lewis, *Mere Christianity* (New York: Macmillan Paperbacks Edition, 1960), p. 87.

2
To Tell the Truth

"Never lie, especially on paper! It can come back to haunt you for infinity, and possibly longer!"

"Sometimes the truth does more damage than good."

The headline over an essay published in *The New York Times* announced: IF YOU'VE EVER FALSIFIED A JOB RÉSUMÉ, READ THIS ARTICLE. A pseudonymous "John Smith" proceeded to describe the time he desperately needed a job and falsely claimed a graduate journalism degree from Columbia University in order to strengthen his application. It backfired when:

1. He was offered the job from among more than 100 applicants.
2. He was asked to bring along proof of his Columbia degree.

"You lied?" the personnel manager said incredulously when "Smith" admitted what he had done. "You just outright lied?" A pause, then: "I'm terribly disappointed!"

"Look," answered "Smith," "I'm not trying to justify what I did. It was wrong and there's no excuse for it. But I qualified for the job because of my experience—and that's real—and you liked my clippings. Besides, lots of people elaborate (I couldn't bring myself to say 'lie') on their résumés."

The personnel manager hesitated, pointed out that it was necessary "to have a relationship of trust" with "Smith" and said to come back the next morning.

"Smith" slept soundly that night, "relieved and reformed," and determined never to lie again on a résumé.

"Sit down, John," said the personnel manager the next morning, looking as though he had had a sleepless night. "I've got a confession to make. Ten years ago, when I was hired here as personnel manager, I lied on my résumé. I claimed I had an M.B.A. degree from Harvard—they never checked. And I've never told a soul—till now."

With one exposure leading to another, "Smith" got the job. He reported that he was then able "to establish a strong relationship of trust" in an organization where "one's degree of competence is not a sheepskin scroll." "Smith's" moral is muddled: apparently blaming his lie on a fetish for degrees. But his example is clear: lying can become a reflex action, even to the point where one social psychologist claims that the average American tells 200 lies a day, including white lies and false excuses of all kinds.

U.S. corporations and businesses certainly are suspicious. They give an estimated 500,000 Americans lie detector tests each year, often as a condition of employment. One-fourth of the country's largest corporations use lie detector tests; one-half of all retail firms and commercial banks require them of job applicants. The public, in turn, is acutely conscious of government lying, particularly since the Watergate scandals. One survey found that 69 percent of all Americans believe that their leaders have consistently lied to them over the past ten years.

Lying leaves everyone uncomfortable, if not indignant. Religiously-concerned Americans are particularly indignant, judging from their responses to situations where lying is an issue in daily life. Lying contaminates and is self-defeating, they point out: "Lying catches up to you in the end" (a Catholic). "Nothing good can be built on lies" (a Lutheran).

But it is easier to condemn lying for out-and-out personal advantage than to condemn lying when there is some justification. Time and again, however, lay Christians agree with moral theologians that extreme care should be taken with the exceptions. Such

9

exceptions are implicit in the definition of lying as "denial of truth to someone who has a right to it." Then the argument shifts to a right to the truth.

"I am not one of those who says you should *never* tell a lie," commented Professor Roger Shinn. "Immanuel Kant says you should not tell a lie to save the life of an innocent person. I *would* tell a lie to save the life of an innocent person. Then the question is: Have I started down the slippery slope so that I'll tell a lie any old time?"

Clearly, those who registered their reactions to truth-telling situations share what Professor Shinn calls his "*strong* predisposition" to truth, as their answers reveal, starting with the matter of falsifying a job application.

In a job application, X writes "attended college for two years" when this is untrue. This is done after a friend at the company says no one will check the statement and it will help in getting the job.

Besides those who simply said WRONG, others who condemned such lying commented that it won't work or will, in the long run, penalize the liar. This was neatly summarized: "Wrong—both from moral and practical reasoning. Morally, it is a lie and practically, it could be very embarrassing down the line."

Variations on the theme of truth or consequences were:

"There may come a time for promotion and no matter what the 'friend' says, the statement could backfire, unless it is a temporary job in X's mind."

"In so doing, the person compromises his honesty. Additionally, later on should the truth be known, this could adversely affect the person's job record and make future job interviews much more difficult."

"Sooner or later, someone will learn the truth and then X will have developed a reputation for lying and won't be trusted."

"X should not do this because if it was found out to be untrue, he would be labeled as dishonest and have no chance of getting the job. If he wrote down that he had no college education, there's still

10

a chance he could get the job. Somehow the truth always comes out."

"It will show in his performance."

"People should be honest. False information only hurts the one giving it in the long run."

"It is illegal to falsify a record. It's just not worth the lie. If he did lie and did get the job because of the lie, he would always feel he was cheating at his work and this might interfere with his performance and self-regard in the future."

Some pointed out that the job-application lie penalizes others, adding injustice to untruth:

"If it helps in getting the job, then it is a gross misrepresentation of the applicant's qualifications. This may cheat both the employer and other more qualified potential employees. Absolutely wrong to lie in this case."

"He is claiming studies and work which others have spent time and money to obtain."

For those who entertained the idea of an exception in this case, the key circumstance was how much the person *really* needed the job. (Of course, each person will define that "need" differently.)

"It really is wrong, but not terribly wrong. I probably wouldn't do it, unless I *really* needed the job."

"It is not right to lie about this. However, if it is the only job available and he has a family to care for, etc., it could be justified as the lesser injustice."

X calls in sick in order to enjoy an extra day off.

"I don't like lies and this is a lie" was a representative answer of those who condemned this practice. Others added these comments: "We have too much of this type of dishonesty at all levels of our society." ... "Should have asked for the day off with the truth." ... "Can you really enjoy the day off after lying?" ... "While not a serious wrong, it is a compromise of one's integrity. If done often, this can become evident to X's superiors in the company."

The dimension of stealing was added: "If you get paid for work

11

you have not done, you would be guilty of stealing from your boss."
. . . "This is an unjust act. The company loses because of absentee-ism."

Those who pointed out that "calling in sick" is accepted prac-tice did not see it as a case of lying. Here, it depends on where an individual works and whether he or she sees it as accepted practice. "An accepted practice so I guess no one considers the statement as true anyway." . . . "This depends on the company or department. In my job, we are encouraged to 'call in sick' if we want a day off."

Seen from the viewpoint of the employee, others accept the practice, regardless of the company's attitude: "If the boss is unrea-sonable, the employee must do it for his sanity." . . . "I agree with this as long as it is not done time after time. People need to have oc-casional rests or surprises (like not having to go to work when you thought you had to). People need a change every once in a while to keep them sane. Call these 'mental health' days."

A Kansas City woman, who noted that "the word *enjoy* has many connotations," tried to take all factors into consideration: "Many businesses encourage employees to do this by refusing to give personal leave days. But more and more businesses are helping employees, who are respected, trusted, valuable assets, and who do not make habits of 'extra days off,' to be able to do this without ly-ing. I feel each person must decide such things for him or herself. I am very happy that I have never had to do this."

A couple are engaged to marry. One of them has had sexual relations during an affair. If it is the woman, should she tell her partner the truth when asked? If the man, should he tell?

Honesty emerges as the best policy for engaged couples re-vealing their past. The reason goes to the heart of marriage:

"Marriage should be based on truth. Both should tell each oth-er about the affair."

"I believe that if either person has had an affair, he should tell the other party. This makes for a better marriage because it would start with trust and honesty."

"If you lie to cover up, you're giving in to a too-restrictive rela-

12

tionship. Spouse of either sex shouldn't expect the other to be a virgin. If this is going to affect the relationship, then it's a pretty phony relationship based on unreal expectations."

"I feel both partners should level with each other at the appropriate time and in the appropriate manner."

"Yes, tell. The past is past, and love conquers all."

While others favor telling the truth about the past, they advise waiting until—and if—asked. The message is: Don't volunteer the information, but don't lie about it—a position based on the significance for the relationship as much as undiluted concern for honesty.

"Both should tell if asked—better to know before marriage and iron out any problems. After marital promises of fidelity, past behavior may look like a *present* violation. Both persons should compare moral questions and responses to see if they see 'eye to eye' regarding a future commitment to faithfulness."

"Both should tell the truth when asked. In such an intimate relationship, candidness is required for a successful future. Untruth now is risky in case that truth is discovered later."

"Should tell the truth when asked, but if not asked should not volunteer the information. Above all, neither should volunteer the information in retaliation or in anger. Also, after such information is exchanged, both parties should either accept the fact and decide to live with it or break the engagement. Then the subject should be shelved forever by both parties."

"If it is the woman, she should tell the man if he asks her directly. He has a right to know. If he should get upset and call the marriage off, then he mustn't have loved her very much and sooner or later he would have found that out. Isn't it better to find out your feelings before you are married? The same goes for the man. What's good for the goose is good for the gander."

Even those who were against telling did not openly favor lying—just withholding the information:

"There is no reason for either one to tell. You can't change the past and the only thing this would do would be to cause suspicion in each one's mind."

"No one should ever tell."

"I do not believe either party has an obligation to tell the other.

13

This may open up a can of worms and cause problems for the marriage in the future."

"Neither should tell."

"I don't think either one should ask the other about these things."

"In both instances, I would say no! What would it add to the relationship? It would be like unloading your guilt on your partner. Forgive yourself and forget it! Go on in your new relationship and never look back."

"I guess my answer would have to be: Why do you ask? If the partner insisted on an answer it would have to be GOODBYE."

A jealous husband is always suspicious of his wife. One day while shopping downtown she meets an old boyfriend and has lunch with him. She decides to lie so her husband won't get upset about what to her is an innocent chance meeting.

A married woman who wasn't certain where she stood was "tempted to write a whole book on this one": "While I would recommend trying to deal with my husband's jealousy through counseling or something of the sort, I don't know that she's obligated to report everything she does. Lying is generally self-defeating and often not necessary when one thinks it is. Usually, lying just puts you under greater restrictions and *prevents* mutual acceptance and forgiveness."

The situation speaks for lies of various shades of white, for lies told with good intentions and for lies told because the other person has no right to the information. The answer, "Sometimes the truth does more harm than good; she may be justified in this case," recalls the rhyming reminder of the English poet William Blake:

A truth that's told with bad intent
Beats all the lies you can invent.

"It may be best to lie," advised another, "just to save her husband undue hurt. As long as she knows it was nothing more than an

14

innocent friendly meeting, she should show her love for her husband in this way."

Others favored the truth largely because a lie wouldn't work and the consequences are worse in the long run because "you always get caught in a lie". . . . "It might start a ruckus in the beginning, but if a lie is told and later found out, hell breaks loose."

"I bet somehow he'll find out, and even if he doesn't, it will come between them. Just her very actions will add fuel to the fire."

"I wouldn't lie about it. But I wouldn't tell the husband unless I was really forced to by him asking point blank or being certain he'd find out about it some other way."

"It is better to tell the truth. It would be better to hear from the wife than someone else who saw them together. Isn't it better to be honest with each other?"

Those who took a hard line toward the husband's jealousy said: "Too bad for him. It's time he grew up. This is her opportunity to tell the truth and help him grow." Or: "I think the husband ought to be challenged in his jealousy. It seems he has never been encouraged to grow up."

When the situation is seen as involving the entire marital relationship, more than lying is at stake:

"First, the issue should probably not be mentioned by the wife unless the husband brings it up. If the issue arises, tell the truth, withhold nothing. If their relationship is not built on trust, it is a weak one. Perhaps more time should be spent on strengthening their love and trust for one another."

"I would suggest that she tell him *nothing* about it. Later on, if necessary, ask him (and everyone else) to help with problems that might arise from this 'chance innocent meeting.' What she *should* do is *refuse* further contact with this 'old boyfriend,' unless she is strong enough to meet anything and everything that could be 'in her immediate and not so immediate' days to come."

"This depends on the extent of the husband's jealousy. If it will start a series of arguments and really cause a lot of trouble, then the wife should not say anything. On the other hand, she might have terrible guilt feelings that could interfere with her attitude toward herself and her husband. If these guilt feelings are very strong, she should confess to her husband, but do it as though it were a casual thing that she shouldn't be guilty for. And then pray."

"She may end up in a fight with her husband, but better she tell him than someone else. If she is honest with him, eventually she may be able to overcome his jealousy or at least teach him to know what 'trust' is and to know that she won't cheat on him. Believe me—I know."

A range of reactions to all the above truth-telling situations was reflected in the comment that none of the situations seemed to be "serious," yet raised the same issue as theologian Shinn's *slippery slope*:

"The insignificant falsehood, which may seem convenient at present, can lead to future complications and the loss of credibility later. Also, if the person develops the habit of choosing false statements for the sake of convenience, he may find it difficult to draw the line when he comes to a more important situation. When a person develops the habit of fabricating the convenient answer, he will have the tendency to do so in all situations."

Father Charles Curran of Catholic University, one of the country's leading moral theologians, put Catholic thinking about lying in historic perspective, then updated it. The older definition indicated lying as wrong because it violated the faculty of speech, which "exists so that I can say on my lips what is in my mind." Even with this clear definition, problems arose: "We can all remember the traumatic experience of what to do when you're age six and your mother tells you to tell the peddler that she's not at home. Well, we had some Jesuit theologians who devised all sorts of broad and strict mental reservations."

But, Curran noted, "today people say that maybe the malice of lying has to be understood in more relational terms." The question is being asked: What is the moral malice of lying? There are different answers: "Lying violates my neighbor's right to truth. But if my neighbor doesn't have the right to truth, then what I sometimes might be forced to say to him is not a lie. Or: lying is action that is not community-building. It's a community-destructive type of action." So he suggests understanding lying in terms of relationships and reponsibilities rather than only comparing what is on the lips with what is on the mind.

16

In approaching the question of lying from the vantage point of a psychiatrist-priest who has examined ethics perceptively, Dr. Ignace Lepp writes of "two temptations" in truth-telling. They represent the extremes of being totally subjective or of being absolutistic: "either to think that the obligation to tell the truth is determined only by personal motives or, secondly, to make the obligation so absolute that it suffers no exception."

Leaving truth-telling totally up to each individual threatens the assumption that we can believe and trust each other. Life together depends on such assumptions and society insists on the right to denounce violations (however numerous they are). St. Augustine goes so far as to warn that "all sin is a kind of lying." On the other hand, to say tell the truth at any cost is to raise the specter of telling the truth to serve a murderous tyrant.

Theologian Shinn cited an example used against Kant's admonition that you cannot tell a lie even to save a life. "You're living under a Nazi regime," he postulated. "You're hiding a Jew and the Gestapo comes to the door asking, 'Is there a Jew in this house?' I'd have no problem of conscience telling a lie. I would say that what forced me to tell a lie was an intolerable moral situation."

In everyday morality, where the choice is not so clear-cut, theologian Shinn worried about the "slippery slope" when I pressed him. Suppose, I asked him, a married seminarian had a jealous wife who phoned and asked if her husband were studying with "Mary." It's an innocent episode, yet the wife is obviously uneasy. His answer revealed the moralist's concern about doing the "right" thing and revealed how much more complicated it is than a question from a Gestapo officer:

> I don't like to waffle on the question, but I would say there are some other things I would try to say first. What they'd be would depend on how well I knew this wife. If I had her confidence, I might say, 'What the heck does it matter? I encourage my students to study together all the time.' I would try to get into that realm of discourse rather than into just a *yes* or *no*. Nonetheless, I hope I'd not tell a lie.
>
> I don't think truth-telling is easy in the sense that it's

just truth or lies, but there *is* virtue in avoiding falsehoods and I try to avoid falsehoods. But, again, do I have a pastoral relation with that wife? Maybe what she is expressing are certain anxieties that I might be able to do something about. Maybe I couldn't, but I'd try to do that as well as answer her question truthfully.

Father McNulty drew on his pastoral experience to underline the value of honesty in a relationship, as with a wife who lies about an innocent chance meeting with a former boyfriend to avoid upsetting her husband. He pointed out in commenting on this "very, very tough question" that a lie can do more damage than good. "She might want to talk out the truth rather than lie if pressed on the matter by her husband. I think that would be a healthier thing. It would be painful to her and they might have some difficult moments, but I'd really like to see her opt for the honest approach for the long-range effect it would have on their marriage. They would then have to talk out how much they trust each other and decide just how much freedom they want to give each other."

Comparing past and current approaches to truth-telling, Father McNulty discussed the other person's right to know: "In the past, we used the term, mental reservation, to cover times when it was better not to tell the truth. A more recent approach is to admit that at times a person does not have the right to the truth or the information you have, particularly if that truth will be harmful to him. Now in this case, it works both ways: a person has no right to know about your extramarital or premarital mistakes and also it's information that would damage the other person and the marriage. So you say, 'No, I didn't do that,' because the other doesn't have a right to that information. It's a judgment that has to be made within that context. This is the area where different judgments may be made, but my pastoral experience prompts me to say: Don't tell the other person."

Theologian Farley took the view that "there are occasions when lying can be justified such as those occasions in which human relations are preserved . . . this might be that kind of case." After commenting that in "*some* situations it would do more harm than good to know the truth," she added her own safeguard against the *slippery slope*:

"There is a strong obligation to tell the truth. It is based in a demand for personal integrity and in the need for trust in interpersonal communication. Yet lying can be justified. The point is that it needs special justification. It is this requirement of *justification* which places a barrier on the 'slippery slope.' You must have overriding reasons which, on balance, show the lie to preserve, rather than destroy, important values."

In any question of lying, Father Curran brought up the matter of personal integrity. It is not so much a matter of whether someone else knows that you have lied—*you know*. Beyond the question of whether anyone else is injured and whether you get what you want: "What does it do to your own moral integrity as a person?"

Here is the basic aversion to lying: what it does to the liar. After that comes concern for what it does to others and to the entire social fabric. Both the moralists and the concerned Christians shared the reactions expressed in one individual's psychologically-probing response:

"What makes people think that they have to lie to others about what they think is correct?"

"What makes people think that someone else's approval is so important that they would have to lie?"

"Can people really live with the lies they tell?"

3

Those Who Help Themselves

"Anything is moral when cheating the phone company!"

"Wrong. The phone company has a right to be paid."

In Burbank, California, the manager of an appliance store explained how he disposes of old stoves turned in by customers: "We take old stoves all the time, even though we can't resell them. If I just put the old range in the alley, it sits there until the trash collectors come. But if I take a crayon and mark a price on the side, it's stolen by the next morning."

In The Inn at Castle Hill in historic Newport, Rhode Island, the newly-arrived guest looks up from the wash basin to see a framed, typewritten message which warns:

"The loss a hotel suffers on towels is unbelievable. Due to this loss, our Housekeeping Dept. has inventoried and signed out towels to your room, with you, the occupant responsible for the same inventory upon checking out:

"2 wash cloths
"2 hand towels
"2 bath towels."

In Cincinnati, a university professor surveyed 100 employees in retail stores and found that 84 felt no guilt in "taking" things from the store without paying for them.

A leading investigator of employee stealing, Mark Lipman, estimates that half of the U.S. work force steals and that one-fourth steal "important items for their own personal use and benefit."

The U.S. Commerce Department provides the kind of staggering governmental estimates that dramatize national problems. Employee dishonesty was estimated at $18 billion for 1977, some $400 million per week—up from only $3 billion ten years before. If that rate of increase continues, dishonest employees will be stealing $1 billion a week by 1983!

Employees are not the only thieves in honest clothes. When all white collar crime is totaled—stealing from the company, and the company stealing from the customer, the client, the government— the larcenous total is an awesome $40 billion a year. That is ten times the annual total resulting from violent crimes against property.

Stealing is like lying. No one has any doubt what it is. But there are differences of opinion about when it is moral to take something or to use something that is not yours. As a rule, the farther away the victim the easier to feel free to steal and the stronger the feelings of hostility the easier to justify actions. This is particularly true amidst the current suspicion of big business, big government, big-time sports, big-anything.

What various individuals particularly resented is being called to honesty in their private lives when corporate and public life is characterized by dishonesty. Along these lines, I recommend the comment of the British novelist, E. M. Forster, in an essay, "What I Believe," written during the precarious prelude to World War II: "As soon as people have power they go crooked and sometimes dotty as well, because the possession of power lifts them into a region where normal honesty never pays. For instance, the man who is selling newspapers outside the House of Parliament can safely leave his papers to go for a drink and his cap beside them: anyone who takes a paper is sure to drop a copper into the cap. But the men who are inside the House of Parliament—they cannot trust one another like that, still less can the government they compose trust other governments."

For those viewing with outrage the way big business operates, that outrage paved the way for exceptions to *Thou Shalt Not Steal*: "My sense of personal morality is easy to compromise when dealing with the corporate state (New York Telephone), which in this case monopolizes and restricts public options when it comes to communicating by phone." . . . "The rates paid at hotels are far beyond the service given. . . ." "The amount of money made by artists and their recording companies is outrageous."

X goes away for a trip and calls home person-to-person, asking for himself or herself so the other party knows of the safe arrival. In this way, there is no charge for the phone call.

On one hand, Americans take the telephone personally as an extension of themselves.

On the other hand, they regard the telephone company as a distant, impersonal giant (sometimes as a giant enemy).

Whenever the phone rings, the everyday is plugged into the corporate conglomerate. Simple one-to-one contacts become dependent on a complex web of bureaucracy, technology, and finance.

Americans who can't live without the phone (as well as a long list of other "necessities," from TV to car to washing machine), are obviously accumulating anger and hostility toward the giant suppliers of their necessities. As things get tougher for the American consumer, the most-hated list will undoubtedly get longer. Various responses bear out what common sense would predict, hostility breeds moral exceptions. "Right on" (as one answer put it) was a pointed reaction to the person-to-person telephone ploy. "Is it wrong?" was asked and answered immediately: "Just take a look at Ma Bell's profits for last year!"

"It's right. System is built on a large profit base!"

"I always would do it."

"I suppose this is wrong. However, as I survey my phone bill and remember certain conflicts I have had with the phone company, it's hard for me to defend Ma Bell."

"Certainly. Why pay? The phone rates are high enough. Ma Bell needs to look at her justice."

"It is wrong, but I would do it anyway. The telephone company rips people off in too many ways."

"Clever. Basically, it isn't right, but since no one is hurt and rates are so high, I don't think it is bad."

"Right. The system makes much more money than it should and this action does not cause any harm."

As in no other question of everyday morality, a number of people admitted they were doing "wrong" without feeling guilty. In calling the behavior "technically wrong on the face of it," one Catholic added: "However, my conscience wouldn't be overly troubled by this action, given the volumes of profit earned by the phone system and given my sizeable lifetime contribution to such a profit."

"It's wrong, but I have done this. I feel that I'm getting even for all the injustices the phone company has done to me. When I try to get them to correct bills, it seems to be always in their favor even if they are *wrong*."

"This doesn't present any problem personally, but I am sure some would say that it would be regarded as cheating, no matter what."

Candid confessions were included: "Wrong. This is cheating the phone company by not paying for the call. I'm sorry to say most people I know do it—including me." "Wrong. Wrong. How many times have I done it? Many!"

However, others who regarded the telephone ploy as wrong could not bring themselves to use it because "it is not paying for service used and in fact is stealing." Variations on this reasoning included: "This is wrong because it cheats the telephone company." "This is wrong because it is still using the services of the telephone company equipment. But because it is a big company people rationalize it as being OK." "Wrong, as the caller is using phone facilities to communicate at no charge for himself."

Even though one parent found that the question has "just given me an idea for gypping the phone company that I never knew about before," the practice was still condemned. "I'm not going to use it nor recommend it to my children who often take trips. I ask them to call collect, and I still will."

Another group argued in favor of taking advantage of the phone company on the grounds that it is not a moral issue. "The need for the person to know the safety of the other person seems to outweigh the cost to public service." "We all use and pay for phone service, hence we would all be subsidizing such use." "I do this all the time. I don't even consider it a moral question to be considered as right or wrong." "Not wrong, as the telephone company tolls are based on the consideration that the person called may not answer and in a certain percentage of instances no tolls will be collected."

Y is staying at a hotel or motel and takes home towels, ashtrays as "souvenirs."

The persistent reaction reflected the strong aversion to stealing, the tangible act of taking what belongs to someone else. "It is stealing," as one person put it, "taking something that does not belong to you. I've heard it rationalized by saying it is built into the hotel or motel's fee, but this does not obscure the fact that you are taking something that does not belong to you."

This theme was expressed repeatedly:

"Property belongs to the motel and you cannot justify taking it for souvenir purposes."

"This can become very expensive to the owners and should be avoided. It's wrong to keep such souvenirs, including the Gideon Bible. They cost someone money."

"Wrong, stealing property which belongs to hotel or motel."

"There is no name for this, except stealing."

In looking at the high rates of hotels and motels, different people came up with different reactions. Some denounced pilfering as one reason for high rates. Others saw the high rates as justification for taking souvenirs. ("Most hotels today, in anticipation of thievery, have added the cost of these items onto the bill. Where this is the case you really should take them because you've paid for them.")

As in a give-and-take, opposing reactions can be paired to illustrate how one person's morality is not another's:

"Wrong. If he keeps doing that, the rates will go up for everyone, even those who do not seek souvenirs. Motel or hotel rates are for the lodging—not for free gifts."

"I always thought these were among the 'perqs' of staying in any hotel. Towels may be going a bit far (who would want hotel towels?), but stationery, soap, etc., are O.K."

"This is an old practice that some take very lightly, but it hurts the public, because it contributes to the inflated rates we have to pay for accommodations today."

"These items are allowed for in hotel and motel expenses, are tax deductible, and provide free advertisement for the hotel or motel. It may be wrong, but it is an encouraged wrong."

"Wrong. This practice is considered by many as 'nothing of consequence.' Yet it is a direct cause, for increased rates as this loss to the owner must be met in some way."

"Such 'walk-away' items are figured in the price of the room! Especially when the hotel has its name on such items. It is advertising, isn't it?"

"Wrong. The rates go up for the next guy."

"Not wrong if they use them for advertising and presume you will take them."

Finally, there was one person's sense of outrage at how hotel/motel pilfering exacts a personal price: "Most hotels and motels plan on people doing it. Therefore, the cost of staying in a hotel or motel is higher. If people would stop stealing, maybe I could afford to travel and stay at a motel!"

Z asks to borrow your record albums in order to tape personal copies instead of buying them.

Between a favor for a friend and the copyright benefits due a distant corporation, a friend has the obvious advantage. He or she is right there and also available to return a favor. Moreover, as was noted: "A lot of people don't realize that copyright law forbids this practice. I wouldn't be in good faith cooperating with the practice. I would have to refuse. It's difficult having to teach morality to another adult. I would give my reason as diplomatically as possible and in some cases would give them the record to play on their phonograph."

No moral issue was seen by many others, including those who felt that buying the record includes the right to lend it to a friend for taping.

"If it was a good friend, I see nothing wrong with sharing. If it was only a mere acquaintance and the only time they called you was to borrow an album to tape it, I would say no."

"Z is more than welcome to them. My purchase of the record gives me the right to use it."

"I can see nothing wrong with this. I would be doing the other person a favor and it certainly wouldn't cost me anything."

"I don't feel there is anything wrong in this as long as the tapes are not for sale, but for that person's own enjoyment."

"I see no problem in taping items in order to save the money it would cost to buy them. It seems stupid to buy a second copy."

"I feel this is OK because it's possible that I might want to do the same."

"This is OK. As long as the tapes are for personal use only. If something happens to the record, I could always borrow Z's tape."

"They could also be taped over radio, TV, etc. No problem as they are practically 'public domain.' "

"Tape recorders were invented to record. If it were wrong, they would not be able to sell recorders."

"Record companies would like to consider this as wrong, but there is a general feeling that you can tape copies for your personal use."

Those who took into account profits of record companies and performers found reason to decide in opposite directions:

"Performers are not starving. In fact they do very well. Recording a record for your personal use (not for sale) is permissible (in fact, I do it all the time)."

"Why not? So, Streisand makes a little less this year!"

On the other hand:

"Wrong. Companies make profits through sales and doing this infringes on another's income."

X makes a habit of taking home office and/or plant supplies for private use—paper, envelopes, building materials, etc.

A little or a lot, with or without employer acquiescence—these facts counted heavily in reactions to this situation. Those who focused on *stealing period* condemned the practice outright:

"Wrong. This isn't part of their job. They are being paid to work and this is stealing."

"Wrong. X is stealing."

"The basic belief by most employees is that taking this sort of supply is not wrong, when in actuality they are stealing."

"Taking things from the office is wrong. The employer supplies these things so we can do our job properly, not to furnish our families with supplies."

"Stealing from an employer on a regular basis is wrong. It's like being paid extra without the employer's knowledge."

"The office and plant supplies were purchased by the company for use by employees in transacting daily business."

"These items do not belong to you and I feel it's wrong to do so. I've told my children also, because I feel it has become a rather large problem in businesses. The primary reason is that it is wrong!"

To support the view that this habit is wrong, a number of people pointed to the consequences to the company, to those who work in the company, and to consumers. "If everyone in the office did this, the company would have to spend more money and eventually cut back services." . . . "Office supplies should only be used for the office. If everyone brought home supplies, the costs would go up for the company and would result in fewer company profits." . . . "I feel that a responsible employee must respect the place he works for. Eventually, the cost of the office supplies must be borne by all and he cheats everyone." . . . "This only contributes to inflationary growth caused by increased operating costs for business. The consumer ultimately absorbs the burden of such increases."

The argument that "it won't be missed" received the following retort: "This sort of self-help system is dishonest in itself and is not extenuated by the supposition that one is only taking from a large and presumably wealthy company which 'will never miss it.' Cost accounting *does* miss the exactions of petty thievery and the practice is so general that it has long ceased to be *petty*. Employee theft is part of the cost of doing business and it is a cost passed on in the prices the company asks for its products, so that ultimately this penalizes X, his relatives and friends, and all of society."

Others took exception to a blanket condemnation of taking things home from the job—when it is minor and when the employer "gives you this privilege." Or where the "employer had knowledge that employees used small amounts of company supplies for their own use and did not specifically condemn this practice orally or in writing." This was interpreted as permission and not judged wrong.

"No big deal, if done occasionally, but not as a regular practice," responded one among those who accepted the taking of minor items: "An occasional pen, pencil, or pad of paper won't hurt. Anything more and I'd feel guilty about it and wouldn't do it." . . . "If of minimal value, O.K. But if the value is substantial, then it amounts to stealing." . . . "I don't think taking these things home is wrong, provided you're not carting out the whole office or supplying your friends and neighbors. I would just consider it a fringe benefit of the job." . . . "Most businesses expect this on a small scale and don't mind. I personally see nothing wrong with this. However, on a large scale, this is definitely wrong and qualifies as theft and is legally punishable."

One parent looked back at her own parents and also looked around at the responsibilities of companies themselves. "I recall being shocked when my father brought home an unopened quart of paint from Con Edison years ago. Never before or after did I see either of my parents take anything. The drugstore man astonished me by telling me how nice my children were—they didn't steal. This set me back on my heels. Obviously, petty pilfering is widespread. On the job, it may be related to working out resentments employees feel for real and imagined grievances, such as low pay. While we're at it, what about company pilfering—bothering employees on lunch hour, overwork and work after 5 p.m., errands to run 'on the way home,' invasions of privacy? Huh?"

This theme was echoed by those who commented that employees sometimes literally take matters into their own hands, as when X "is underpaid and takes home materials as his way of getting even for being underpaid."

Pushing aside all these considerations, one direct response rejected any exceptions: "The only thing I make a habit of taking home is my paycheck."

In condemning stealing, the moral theologians took pains to identify the act of taking what is someone else's as the problem, whatever its worth. Father McNulty ticked off each situation and its relationship to honesty:

On "beating" the telephone company: "I have the feeling that many people see this as fun. They seem to get a kick out of 'beating' the telephone company. When people talk to me about it, I see a twinkle in their eyes which says they do it more for fun than for the dollar or two they save. It is only a small thing, but it is dishonest. You're cheating the phone company. I think it is one of the subtle ways in which we let dishonesty creep into our lives."

On taking things from hotels and motels: "You're certainly not doing something gravely wrong, but it is a form of stealing. I really don't think that hotels and motels tolerate the taking of 'souvenirs.' It's particularly unfortunate if children are along and see the family doing it. It can create a tendency to steal when it seems 'safe.' "

On taping record albums: "It looks to me to be dishonest, since you're hurting people who make a living by putting out records."

On bringing supplies home from work: "Making a habit of it is what's wrong. It is making a habit of stealing."

In commenting on the person-to-person ploy, Father Richard A. McCormick of Georgetown University saw an attitude problem. He commented that the telephone company "can easily circumvent this if they wanted to do so" by imposing a small charge on all attempts to make phone calls. (Something like this is actually done in the Scandinavian countries.) Since the telephone company doesn't choose to do this in the United States, he is not concerned about the moral issue, but about an "attitudinal problem—getting something for nothing." However, when one Catholic theologian heard of this view, he felt that Father McCormick had "skirted the issue completely," demonstrating once again that morality depends on how a situation is viewed.

Just as lying raises the issue of the other person's right to know, stealing raises the question of the other person's right to grant permission, whether it involves taking things from hotels/motels or

29

from an employer. Not everyone sees "permission" in the same way, as was evident in the answers of various individuals, but clearly "permission" counts in deciding the morality of "helping" yourself to property and services.

Professor Milhaven noted that it makes a difference if minor items in huge supply are taken and "if the company expects it." He added that "a great deal depends on custom in a particular company, though this can be abused." Or as Father McCormick remarked: "It's stealing, unless there is tacit acquiescence as company policy." In calling the practice wrong "ordinarily," Father Curran said it is another matter "if it is tolerated and everyone else is doing it."

As to taping record albums, the issue rests on what Father Curran cited as the "author's right to the fruits of his or her own labor and the copyright laws enforce this right." Father O'Connell and Father McCormick cited the obligations to honor the law, which is legitimately applied to copyright situations. Even here, Father Curran pointed to a possible difference in interpretation: "If you think that the author is being unreasonably paid, then you could argue it's O.K."

In the final analysis, the moralists were concerned about Professor Shinn's "slippery slope." As with lying, they were troubled about "harmless stealing" becoming a habit, and then a way of life.

4
Taking Advantage

"As my mother used to say: 'Would you jump off the Empire State Building if your best friend was doing it?' Just because others cheat doesn't make it right."

"I do not know. . . . I'd probably cheat (if others were planning to cheat)."

In the famous slogan of America's ultimate jock, football coach Vince Lombardi, "winning isn't everything; it's the only thing."

In the view of America's ultimate philosopher, William James, a "moral flabbiness" is "born of the exclusive worship of the bitch-goddess SUCCESS." He called it "our national disease," along with "the squalid cash interpretation put on the word success."

Winners presume losers.

Success presumes failure.

Both involve competition, which is the *real* American pastime, from cradle to coffin. Infants are compared with one another and toddlers soon get the message that they are better (looking, behaved, loved, etc.) than siblings, cousins, etc. The old get buried and the mourners look out the corner of their eyes to register the quantity of flowers, size of cortege, and location in the cemetery.

Americans get a double message: on one hand, winning and succeeding are what count; on the other hand, how you play the game and live your life *really* count. Clichés carry the double message:

Everyone should try to be successful. . . .

But the kind of person you are is more important than being successful.

Money isn't everything. . . .

But money talks. (Or, in a mocking reversal of another cliché: Health isn't everything; it can't buy money.)

For Christians, Jews, and humanists, the Golden Rule calls the signals when they compete, and guides their play. In trying to succeed, don't do unto others what you wouldn't want them to do to you. Don't take unfair advantage. Don't cheat.

The Golden Rule is readily proclaimed in the best of all possible worlds. But in the actual world, others do cheat and put at a disadvantage those who don't cheat. Cheating emerges even in kindergarten games and comes on strong with the first school examination. Its shadow looms, from school to job, from card table to tennis court. As long as winning and succeeding matter, taking advantage is a problem—for those tempted to do it, for those tempted to do it to stay even with those who do, and for those tempted to benefit from the tactics of others.

A college student faces a major examination that could jeopardize a much-needed scholarship. Illness has prevented proper preparation for the exam, but the professor rejects any excuses. So the student decides to cheat.

Repeatedly, a strong aversion to cheating produced the single-word response: WRONG. Those who explained their reaction against cheating in the exam were emphatic:

"Cheating is never justified no matter how 'noble' the reason."

"There is never an excuse for cheating. Everyone has problems, but cheating doesn't solve anything."

"Wrong. In the end, you are the one who is cheated."

"Cheating doesn't gain anything."

"On the *chance* that he might not do well on the exam, he *definitely* 'fails' by cheating. How would he feel about a scholarship he won by cheating? It would negate all his hard efforts previously. Be honest!"

In trying to put the situation in perspective, one midwesterner

32

commented that "while the scholarship is much needed, it isn't the end of the world." This was echoed by: "He should have more faith in his ability. There are many obstacles in life."

When the situation was complicated by adding that "several students are planning to cheat on the exam," the objectors held firm: "Cheating is still wrong." . . . "It's still wrong for the same reason." . . . "Still no." . . . "It would be tempting, but I would still go on my own merits." . . . "He must live with his conscience." . . . "He still shouldn't cheat. If he does, he is only cheating himself."

Those who were not so certain commented:

"I would go above the professor to try to work something out. Tempting to cheat, though, if no one wants to help."

"It's probably wrong to cheat, yet I might, depending on other factors."

"I'm not so clear on this, though I never cheated on any test. But then I never put any value on grades whatsoever."

The argument in favor of cheating focused on the professor's "unreasonable" attitude as justification:

"If the professor rejects excuses and is unreasonable, he almost deserves to have the student cheat. Of course, it's wrong, but with all these pressures perhaps you have to do what you have to do! But can you live with yourself knowing you did it?"

"Since the professor is unfair, the student should have no guilt feelings for his actions."

For a recent college graduate, distance added perspective: "I would probably have felt the same if I had been ill. It seems like a legitimate excuse. However, after thinking about it, I would never have cheated."

So much for situations where cheating involves someone else's rating of you. In other situations, the individual provides information which, in turn, affects the outcome of competition.

Employee performance in X's company is rated every four months as the basis for promotions and raises. Employees supply some of the information themselves; several exaggerate in what they report. X is trying to decide whether to exaggerate in order to stay competitive.

"Exaggeration," in the view of a Kansan, "is a fancy word to gloss over a lie" and so it's "wrong," a view shared by many Christians:

"It would be morally wrong to exaggerate. Just because others exaggerate it would not be right for X to exaggerate also."

"It would be wrong to exaggerate. However, he should give himself full credit for the situations in which he deserves merit, not belittling his efforts nor exaggerating them. His honest appraisal will be recognized among the others."

"I wouldn't exaggerate. I would let my own merits speak for themselves."

"X must be honest. It won't help to exaggerate. God knows what he's done. He himself knows what he's done."

Yet, as one churchgoer commented, "there is a fine (and difficult) distinction between putting things in their best light and exaggerating to the point of lying. One should try to do the former while avoiding the latter." Along similar lines: "What is exaggeration? I would certainly try to put my best attributes down, but I am not sure how many of my faults I'd put down. There is no such thing as an objective report of anything."

A major argument against exaggeration focused on the practical rather than the moral aspect: "Exaggeration will show up in the person's performance and will embarrass him." ... "In time, the employee would have to meet expectations." ... "The company's bosses probably have a pretty good idea of what's going on. Once you exaggerate a lot and you're known for this, people are cautious about believing whatever you say!" ... "Your own self-respect should be more important. In the end, exaggeration may be cause for dismissal, demotion, and embarrassment if employees are unable to perform at the expected level."

While outright lying was rejected, the main view in favor of exaggeration was exemplified by this response: "Right, because exaggeration is common and accepted and not to do it would be a severe handicap. Again, I emphasize exaggeration and not out-and-out lying."

Both moral sensitivity and the competitive sense were joined by the comment, "hard choice," followed by: "To be honest with yourself or not is the way I view the decision. Not to exaggerate would keep peace of mind, but in business that could mean staying low man if the company wants aggressiveness."

A salesman is expected to give buyers cash gifts under the table and to make up for the money by padding his expense account.

Besides denouncing this practice as wrong, a number of people offered advice: get another job: "Wrong! No way! If this is a part of the job, someone else should have it—not I." . . . " 'Forcing' the giving of gifts and 'forcing' their being made up by padding an expense account is putting pressure to do wrong. I would seek other employment." . . . "This is dishonest. I suggest he find a different job." . . . "As an industrial salesman, I can honestly say that not only is this immoral, but it is utterly unnecessary and self-defeating. I would quit this job immediately or at least make clear to my boss what my position is."

A woman reported her husband's experience: "This did actually happen to my husband. He lost the account, but they now have a different buyer who again is buying from my husband and to date is purchasing more."

A minority tended toward acceptance of the practice, beginning with the comment that the practice is "understandable" and "accepted": "If it is the accepted way, you must compete or get out. It is only right because his superiors know and approve."

When the situation was altered by adding family responsibilities and threat of job loss, the objections to "payoffs" became stronger, rather than weaker.

(Suppose the same salesman—a father of four—has been warned his job is in jeopardy because of low sales. A buyer promises a big order if the salesman makes a payment under the table and certifies that 10% of the shipment is defective so the buyer can get a refund.)

One immediate response was "Here we go too far. It is now time to get out." Others responded: "Once you give in to this kind of temptation, you have opened the door to do it over and over and your resistance will decrease accordingly. Perhaps, he could talk to his boss about possible alternatives—a different territory or product line." ... "If I had to stoop to this kind of tactic, I would have to wonder if I am in the right business and maybe I would look for another job." ... "Through experience, *not* through moral preparation, I can say that if you think this sort of thing actually *gets* sales, you're an *incompetent* salesman and ought to look for another job immediately before you're fired. I'm not sure that I would be so emphatic if I didn't have my own business experience."

The family responsibility of four children was open to two different interpretations. One person could "see how someone with four children could be really upset enough to accept this kind of a deal. He needs the job and could be desperate." Another noted that the action is "unethical and he does have four children to set an example for."

Next, how to behave on the receiving end of special payments, as in this case:

Two travel agents of equal qualifications bid for your company's travel business. One agent promises to make it worth your while if he gets the contract. Which one do you pick?

Repeatedly, the offer of "making it worthwhile" backfired by putting the agent in an unfavorable light: "Pick the one who did *not* make a promise. If not for moral reasons, then because it's smart business to do business with the more honest." ... "The other agent, I feel he would perform honestly." ... "I wouldn't pick the one who offered to make it worth my while. Since he's that underhanded, he would probably expect something from me later on." ... "One doesn't get something for nothing. If the one agent is going to 'cheat' on his company, don't you suppose you are going to 'get it' someplace else down the line. Contracts should be straightforward and aboveboard."

Others wanted to know more, making it clear the case is not open and shut. "This is a tough one! I think you should have elaborated more. Is this gift deceitful or is it something I could share with others in my company? Many companies offer incentives to buyers." ... "I would pick the one that I thought would give me the best service over a long-term period. It wouldn't necessarily be the one that makes the offer (bribe)." ... "Humanly, you go with the one making the offer. Morally, you should go with the other. I personally would tend to go with the one I liked best, which would probably be the one not offering anything." ... "Find out what he means by 'worth your while.' If not right, choose the other agent."

All things appearing equal, some readily chose the travel agent offering the "extra": "If the travel agent is going to give me part of his commission to get the business and is not hurting his company, I'd take the best deal." ... "Probably pick the one making it worth my while, unless my choice of this particular agent is helping to put the other out of business." ... "I would pick the one who would make it worth my while."

The responses of moral theologians spotlighted the "rules of the game." Theologian Farley emphasized the principle of fairness: "You have no right to take unfair advantage of others." She included situations in which self-defense can be offered as a justification for cheating: others are doing it and to avoid being placed at an unfair disadvantage, cheating is necessary. Her response:

"By and large, I say no. Competition always takes place within a limited context, which is like a game with rules. Once you join in the 'game,' you can't start rewriting the rules, even though other people are doing it. That, of course, does not mean that (a) the individual rules of the game should never be challenged in terms of whether they are morally fitting or that (b) the whole game should never be challenged even from within."

Responding along similar lines, Father McNulty reasoned that cheating on an exam is not justified by the fact that others are cheating. With regard to the salesman, he called attention to a policy some businesses have of giving a bonus or an "extra" to someone who is buying from them. But he regarded the idea of padding an expense account as a lie involving dishonesty.

While not disagreeing, Father Curran discussed exceptions to the rules. He compared these cases to discussions about multinational corporations which bribed foreign officials in order to make sales. He cited the "justification that this is the way of life over there, this is what everybody does and we cannot put our company at an unfair disadvantage." His comment can be misinterpreted if looked at in isolation: "I can see that as a valid argument."

He added two points:

1. "I'm not saying you should do it, but you could." (Here, he included the possibility of deciding to cheat on an exam.)

2. Beware of convenient rationalizations, of going along simply because everyone is doing it.

People caught in an immoral situation not only keep it going, but maintain its immorality by joining in. At the same time, reasonable survival tactics could call for going along, even taking advantage to avoid disadvantage.

As Father Curran talked about the specific situations involving competition, he raised questions which challenged easy rationalizations:

Of the salesman forced to pay under the table: "Maybe I'm romantic or idealistic, but is the system basically that corrupt? Is it true that everybody is doing it? I'm not so sure that's the case."

Of the father of four faced with the prospect of paying off to make a sale: "Everyone has to be aware of one's responsibilities to one's children, but in this case there is the possibility of changing jobs, etc."

Curran also warned about "the danger of rationalization," a theme repeatedly raised by moral theologians as they refrained from telling people how to behave and focused on the individual's responsibility to make moral decisions—conscientiously, carefully, and with concern for as many dimensions as can be taken into account.

A liberation theologian like Dr. T. Richard Snyder of New York Theological Seminary looked at everyday morality in terms of the whole society and basic human needs. While coming from a tradition different from that of Catholic theologians, his comments were not as different as they may have seemed at first. He sounded more ready to allow exceptions to the standard rules of expected behavior, but he placed a heavy moral responsibility on each individual who makes an exception:

"In every case where someone makes an exception to what is considered acceptable or standard morality, he or she takes on the responsibility of working to change the system, to make it more just."

In other words, breaking the rules is moral only in context and in terms of accepting the responsibility to work for justice, a view in keeping with his approach to morality:

"As a liberation theologian, I am committed to principles like justice, making life more human, meeting the basic needs of people, recovery of the erotic and joyful dimensions of life that have been lost. These principles inform any decision.

"Many of these cases would be falsely dealt with only as individual decisions. Obviously, the individual is responsible for a decision, but these individual decisions are set within a matrix that has to be understood. For me, that matrix is the question of who have power, what they are doing with power, what is being done to those without power by those with power."

Dr. Snyder described himself as a Presbyterian rooted in the Calvinistic tradition, "a rich resource for understanding what it means to stand over and against power structures that are unjust." "I also have a strong rooting in the whole line of Baptist and radical reformation tradition and in the prophetic tradition of the Old Testament," he added.

So for him, taking advantage is not acceptable simply as getting even or getting your own. Breaking rules can involve physical or psychological survival, where the individual is in on the low end of a power relationship and being done in. Here the Snyder view of everyday situations is not far from that of the other moral theologians. They talk of needing more details and they leave the door open to breaking the rules under certain conditions—which for each individual amounts to how he or she sizes up the situation and interprets its conditions. The result is not only a moral decision in personal and subjective terms. It exemplifies the legitimate difference already mentioned by Father Curran.

Here are Dr. Snyder's reactions to the specific situations:

"Under the extreme circumstances of a competitive situation in which the student *really* did not have fundamental choice and the professor is exercising extreme rigidity, the student has a right to make some decision to cheat if he has to stay alive in the situation— if there is no other recourse. On the other hand, if this student makes it through, then the student bears a responsibility to attempt changes or at least to work against the competitive mentality.

"I would reject kickbacks or cheating done solely for personal aggrandizement and here the individual needs a community of others to help see whether that is the case. Such behavior could be legitimate for survival reasons, but we must realize that every time we break the law we, in fact, have done something that is at least ambivalent or ambiguous in terms of its implications for our moral lives."

He zeroes in on the notion of manipulation and views American society as manipulative: "These illustrations refer to manipulative actions on the part of victims who are themselves subject to a larger power manipulating them constantly. These then can be actions to protect their own ego, to protect their survival and, in some cases, hopefully to develop solidarity with others working to develop a countervailing power."

By now, immersion in the thinking of moral theologians and of lay Christians shows that there is a moral place for breaking rules—but not lightly, easily, or freely. Rather than rationalize rule-breaking, the moral theologians are in the business of sensitizing the individual to the moral dimensions of a decision.

5
Beating the System

"Wrong. He is buying a favor and claiming undue special privilege."

"If no one is inconvenienced by this, I don't see the harm."

A self-employed cab driver and a suburban matron in a white Cadillac pinpointed life under the *system* during a gas shortage. He had to tip a gas attendant in order to get enough gas to operate his taxi in downtown Washington, D.C. She parked in front of her Westchester gas station after the pumps were closed to the general public, greeted the owner, and casually got out of her car so he could drive her car to the pump for a super-unleaded tankful.

One person's privilege is another's necessity.

Both were "beating the system," the established rules for getting things done, the way things are supposed to work, the regular order of business. Both were plugging into the other *system*, the unwritten way things get done by adjusting, manipulating, and breaking the rules to gain advantages and/or remove disadvantages. In every society, there are people who never wait on line, always get the best seats, the lowest prices, the inside track. For some, "beating the system" is a matter of survival, for others a matter of comfort. For some, a source of pride, for others a matter of convience, and for some others a key to making ends meet. There are also many concerned Christians for whom the notion is all wrong, even when moralists can point out mitigating circumstances.

41

A private bargain is made with justice. It can be an occasional reach for preference or advantage or can be built into a way of life, of doing business. Some years ago when *Life* magazine ran a series on "Crime in the U.S.," a plausible summary of a day in the life of a "typical" businessman catalogued the byways of "beating the system." In a composite day, the "reputable" businessman:

Left his car in a No Parking zone and greeted the veteran cop on the beat, who thanked him for his recent annual present, a case of whisky (penalty for attempting to influence a police officer with a gift: $5,000 fine and/or 10 years in jail).

Consulted his personal tax advisor on how to distort repair and depreciation costs in order to avoid taxes (penalty for fraudulent income tax return: $10,000 fine and/or five years in jail).

Entertained his wife and two personal friends at a lavish lunch on the company expense account (misdemeanor subject to $500 fine and/or one year in jail).

Reminded an assistant to "take care of" a building inspector to cut red tape at a new building site (penalty for bribing a public officer: $5,000 fine and/or 10 years in jail).

Dictated a letter thanking a supplier for his gift of a new model portable TV set (penalty for secretly accepting a gift in return for corporate favors: $500 fine and/or one year in jail).

Congratulated his company controller for a bookkeeping device that inflated company assets (penalty for concurring in a bookkeeping fraud: $500 fine and/or one year in jail).

Before the businessman sat in front of his souvenir TV set to fume at the crimes reported on the 11 o'clock news, *Life* added other items: approved a misleading TV commercial, took home a company desk set for his den, advised his wife to ignore Social Security payments for the maid. So ran a day at work, at home, and at large, a series of encounters with law and license, obligation and advantage, restrictions and manipulations.

"Unless a person is well-grounded in faith *and* has others who love him and will listen to him," commented one exercised Catholic, "he becomes more and more bitter, especially in middle age. Or he joins the system and 'gets what is his.' A third course is withdrawal, either into a different occupation or into oneself—which can include complete or nearly complete rejection of the world, as I've seen happen."

Withdrawal is not realistic, if really possible. While we can escape a particular system, we can't escape systems, including those of our own making. That means rules which guide actions and thereby set apart the acceptable and the unacceptable, the "good" and the "bad." Everyday life constantly brings us face-to-face with situations which tempt us to:

Avoid the consequences of rule-breaking;
Compensate for "unfair" application of the rules;
Take advantage of rules.

Businessman, woman in a white Cadillac, cabdriver, everyone has a life to make, balancing the guidelines inside with the rules outside. Some cases in point:

A store owner gives his building inspector $10 a month to avoid a summons under obsolete regulations. If he receives a summons, he will end up losing half a day in court and pay a $25 fine.

Y's son faces suspension of his driver's license for an accident. The son is a safe driver who needs the car for his job. A lawyer friend says: "I can take care of the case. Just give me three $100 bills and don't ask any questions."

The thought of bribery to avoid the consequences was hard to swallow, as reflected in this pair of answers:

"Obsolete regulations may be 'hard to take,' but until they are changed, they are the regulations to be obeyed. The store owner might investigate how to change the regulations instead of transacting illegally with the inspector. A day in court may be a beneficial place and time to voice the problems with the regulation."

"Safe driver or not, all accidents are to be reported. The other party involved may be cheated out of his rights by not going

43

through the proper channels. Paying the $300 is bribery or a payoff and is wrong—for *any* reason."

A similar reaction: "I disapprove of bribery—however well-motivated."

An added reason for not paying the money to help the son was cited: "Wrong. Very bad example to give a son. Proper courses can be followed in making an appeal. Until then, another way will have to be found for the son to go to work. One has a responsibility to help and teach the child in the correct way." . . . "Wrong. The father is teaching his son that money can buy you anything and that it's OK to do something as long as you don't get caught. And if you do get caught, there's always a way to cover your mistake."

For others, the lawyer was the target of criticism, a candidate for exposure to the bar association and to the courts. "This builds distrust in lawyers," said one churchgoer. "I'd be afraid to deal with him in solving my problems."

A different approach placed the "burden on the lawyer who perhaps knows of legal loopholes," thereby closing one's eyes toward the prospect of bribery.

An argument in favor of paying a bribe to the building inspector ran this way: "He cannot fight city hall. What is wrong is the system, as the inspector would probably find a violation every month anyway. There should be an obligation on the part of the store owner to unite with others and fight the building department if he has the ability. The system is at fault in such cases."

> **In filing an insurance claim for a fire that damaged his kitchen, X pads the reimbursement claim to make up for a previous claim that X feels was unfairly rejected.**

> **Z is convinced a raise was denied unjustly. To make up for it, Z pads an expense account for an average $15 per week—the equivalent of the raise.**

The temptation is to balance the scales of justice. The argument against padding the insurance claim centered on treating each claim separately instead of maintaining a long-range accounting system. The argument against padding the expense account was more direct: it's stealing.

Specific comments on the insurance case were:

"X should have protested the first claim instead of padding the second. It would have made him feel better and he wouldn't have to lie on the second."

"Wrong. X should stick to the claim at hand, ignoring what injustices he may have perceived in the past."

"No. Each claim should be settled on its own merits. One injustice does not compensate for another."

"Wrong. You are entitled to what policy says and if they said no, I'd be aggravated, but accept it and just hope for best on next."

"Wrong to pad a second claim. One should not sign for the first claim until one is satisfied with the adjustment. There is a proper course of action to get what one believes is fairly his. If one was ignorant or too lazy to do so, that does not give the right to cheat later."

One wife commented that while she could not do this, her husband would "feel justified in doing this and I probably would have to go along with him whether I wanted to or not."

To the employee who makes up for a raise that was not granted, a twofold message was sent: padding the expense account won't work in the long run and anyone who does it is confirming that he or she doesn't deserve a raise. ("He's showing why he was rejected. He's stealing.")

"He may not have gotten a raise," one commentator said, "but he also may not have a job if his boss finds out. I doubt the risk is worth it."

Or: "Wrong. Eventually Z would be found out. If the expenses are checked into, then he would be embarrassed and he certainly wouldn't be ahead of the game." . . . "Hope he doesn't get caught. Might be denied his job, too."

Taking a larger view than the individual situation, one response was: "A person has to live with himself or herself." Another disapproved, commenting that "if a society is to become more just, it must begin with each person."

Would you ask a friend working in a department store to buy something for you at employee discount?

A sports fan buys a low-priced ticket for the big game and then gives an usher $5 in order to sit in a high-priced seat.

In situations where individuals take the initiative in taking advantage, friendship complicates. They hesitate to impose on their friends, but they don't take organizations personally. And once again, consumer outrage surfaced, as in the response of a midwest Lutheran who was uncompromising on all situations, except in the matter of tipping to get a better seat: "Seats are overpriced. In situations like this, management gets what it deserves."

Others focused on the fact that the seat was empty: "If no one has taken the seat and the usher is agreeable, I suppose it is okay. After all, the seat is vacant and the game probably would be in progress in order for the usher to do this. But I myself would not do it."

"That higher priced seat had to be vacant. The usher is only selling the favor of directing the fan to a vacant higher-priced seat. He is not selling the seat."

"Why not? The seat would go unoccupied anyway."

The same man who would readily tip in order to get a better seat would have no part of getting an employee discount through a friend at a department store: "It's a bare-faced dishonest act." Another commented: "The discount option is only for employees, which I am not." Even when offered such a discount by friends, a third person reported refusing: "I don't like the practice."

This attitude was reinforced by concern about "taking unfair advantage of a friendship" and "straining a close relationship." Another was concerned about "an imposition on the friend." The store, as well as the friend, added up to *no*: "I would not want to embarrass my friend nor cheat the store."

The view that "the store is not losing anything or they wouldn't give the discount" left others feeling free to ask a friend for the discount. Resentment against high prices made it more acceptable: "Certainly! Department stores make a remarkable markup on even the employee discount. They won't miss it."

Feelings ran strongest in confronting the system of unemployment compensation. Collecting such compensation while earning money on the side regularly raises cries of "chiseling" in newspapers. Economists cite a vast underground economy built on unreported income. Sociologists dissect a phenomenon that has the features of both conventional and white collar crime, but does not fall neatly into either category. Moralists ponder when it is ethical to collect jobless pay while earning money. Meanwhile, the unemployed juggle the pressures of inflation, personal and family needs, and the risk of breaking the law. Here is the case in point presented to concerned Christians:

W is receiving unemployment compensation, but works on the side for cash and does not report the income. W says the extra money is needed to support self and family.

The reactions divided between those who looked primarily to the law and those who looked mainly to the situation facing the unemployed person. On one hand: "Another conniving rascal who ought to know better." On the other hand: "Everyone does this. (Of course, this doesn't mean it is 'right.') Personally, I would not even need the added justification of supporting 'self and family.'"

Cheating and breaking the law predominated in the views condemning those who beat the system of unemployment compensation:

"Wrong. This is breaking the law. The income should be reported."

"This is cheating—even though the money may be needed. While I would sympathize with the man, I feel what he is doing is wrong."

"This person should use the time in an effort to secure full-time employment."

"Wrong. Stealing."

"Costs the taxpayer like crazy. Hate it."

"This person is one of many—probably the majority. But his dishonesty hurts others. Funds for relief of crises, such as unemployment, are very tight. When one person takes more than his due from such a pool, it inevitably means that others faced with the same crisis get less than their due. The span of unemployment compensation could probably be lengthened by a couple of weeks if everyone reported the income from their jobs on the side."

With varying degrees of acceptance, others focused on the situation facing the unemployed person. Some said it was all right *if* the jobless payments are not high enough; several assumed they are not: "Unemployment compensation is not enough to live on. A person should do anything possible to support himself or his family." ... "I don't see anything wrong with this, since I know that the money received for unemployment compensation isn't a full salary. And it does take so much to live." ... "Seeing the amount of money unemployment provides, I condone the extra non-reported income. There is hardly any reasonable way to support a family on unemployment insurance."

Working on the side was even described as more than morally tolerable. It was praised: "Today, 'society' is setting people up to have to do what they wouldn't do otherwise. If you can get unemployment compensation and can also earn a bit of cash, it's OK. Why bury your talent? Also, why bury your incentive?"

A balancing act was at work, as set forth in the reaction: "Although the income is supposed to be reported, the higher priority of need would seem to make this OK, if not totally right."

The moral theologians also balanced principles and faced up to compromise in what is not the best of all possible worlds. In the beginning, theologian Farley suggested that we come to terms with the fact that systems are inescapable: "You cannot live apart from them." Systems involve real other people and "beating the system" is not a matter of just getting around the rules. It can mean penalizing other people. So: "You have to ask yourself whether the system has any claims; what 'system' means, whether system is in fact just an abstraction and therefore won't have any claims or whether it stands for concrete people who do have claims over and against my claim."

The trust factor is also present, she added: "If I am always out

48

to beat the system, that means there can be no system that could at all be based on my trust. One has to consider whether that is the sort of world you want to live in and whether you are going to foster such a world."

A further complication arises in confrontations with systems: whether the system is just or unjust. Here is the area where conscientious Christians felt free to break the rules when they rejected a system as unjust and therefore not binding. In theologian Farley's words: "I might perceive the system to be basically unjust; then it in itself cannot settle all questions of competing claims."

These were the common threads woven into the reactions of both conscientious Christians and moral theologians when Monday morality met the system: fairness to others, trust, justice (involving both individual action and particular system). What Father Curran called "rough"—rather than ideal—justice emerges. Also differences of opinion.

Father McNulty felt that paying off the building inspector "just can't be done," but he did raise the possibility of a "proportionate reason" for helping a son out of the license jam. Whereas Dr. Snyder would not help his own son or daughter in the latter situation, he would pay the building inspector $10 each month. To do justice to their variations, here is their reasoning:

Father McNulty: "I feel that the real evil in the license case is the effect on the son and what the father is teaching him. I would hate to think that the son feels he can do what he wants and have it 'fixed up.' By taking away the realization of the penalty and its use as a deterrent, the father might harm the son more in the long run. If the son absolutely needed the job, you might talk about proportionate reason for paying the lawyer to take care of the case, but I would like to know much more about the circumstances."

Dr. Snyder: "One thing that strikes me here is the whole question of public transportation. Why should anyone need to have a car in order to get to a job, unless one were a traveling salesman. The question of a suspended license obviously would depend on the circumstances. If it's not a survival question, then I don't know that I'd be so quick to say that the father should do this. If one of my two daughters or my son were involved, I think I would say, 'No, you have to find another way to get to your work.'

"If I were the store owner, I would probably pay the building inspector the $10 to avoid losing the inordinate amount of time as a victim of an obsolete rule. I would prefer to use the time saved in not going to court to get City Hall to change the rule."

"There is such a thing as an unjust law," Father Curran commented, "and unjust laws don't oblige. But the problem is in bribing someone. You're contributing to a situation in which bribery is an accepted thing in public morality and you are maintaining a corrupt system. We had in Washington two fires—one in a nursing home, one in a halfway house—where the building inspector had not required the necessary safety devices. People died as a result. So you cannot tell the long-range as well as immediate consequences of contributing to a corrupt system."

On the question of not reporting income while receiving unemployment compensation, the moral theologians were more sympathetic than those who denounced the practice. But they insisted on a qualifying condition: whether the income was needed to maintain what Father Curran called "frugal comfort." "If an individual or family is forced to live below the poverty line as established by the government, then a case can be made for not reporting the income," he added. Professor Milhaven said it is not necessary to report such income if unemployment insurance is not adequate. But this does not apply if it is "a matter of convenience."

Theologian Farley reasoned that "there is something so grossly inadequate about our system that there are instances where it is justified not to report such income when people cannot live otherwise." Then, "justice calls for what we would otherwise call stealing." She drew a parallel with the oft-quoted case of Thomas Aquinas: taking food to avoid starvation from someone who can spare it. "The underlying principle here is that property rights are qualified by basic human needs for survival."

Surveying the problem of dealing with systems in general, she added, however, that it's a "mistake" to think that the only way of dealing with unjust systems is getting around them. "To some extent, our integrity can be compromised. We can become evil like the system in order to beat it; whereas, if the system is unjust, it ought insofar as it is possible to be challenged in other ways than in getting around it in hidden ways."

50

In particular, Dr. Shinn cited the moral approach in which "no person should be a judge in his or her own case." The disgruntled employee who didn't get a raise and the policyholder making up for a rejected insurance claim are both judging their own cases. The difficulty, Dr. Shinn added, is that so are the employer and the insurance company acting as their own judges. Quite frankly, he noted, people would admit that getting even in such cases is wrong, then might go ahead and do it.

Where a department store and a sports organization enter the picture, Father McNulty advised taking into account the policy in effect. Some stores explicitly stipulate that employees should use their discount only for themselves and the members of their family. That rules out using an employee discount for a friend. Others are vague and don't object, even expect their employees to do this. That's the crucial piece of information to obtain from a friend. At the ballpark when a fan notices an empty seat and tips the usher to sit there, that may be considered part of what the usher is allowed to do. But Father McNulty distinguishes between someone who does this "casually" and occasionally and someone who does it regularly.

Father McNulty echoed what concerned the moral theologians repeatedly: "What I dislike most about such situations is plugging into a whole system that says you can buy anything you want, where everyone is on the take, where as long as you pay you can do anything you want. It's corrupting for the whole society. The more we give into that, the more we partake of it, the more we contribute to the evil that's in the world."

The concept of occult compensation came up in discussing cases where individuals beat the system. Each person drawing up his or her own moral ledger can decide to balance the accounts with individual rule-breaking. Such do-it-yourself moral accounting runs the danger of self-delusion, or self-serving judgments that unfairness and injustice justify breaking the rules.

As a traditional moral concept, occult compensation applies to situations where an individual has no other way of obtaining the compensation due him or her, except to take it secretly. "But," as theologian Kenny explained, "for the individual in the average situation, this is neither desirable nor permitted. Nor does it make sense on a wide scale for society. When individuals are working out private arrangements with their consciences rather than confronting the injustices in society and in working situations, injustice is perpetuated. Taking a stand against injustice is more beneficial for the individual and for society, rather than the attitude which says: 'I'll accept this situation and then make it up on the side by secretly taking advantage of opportunities to make it up myself without anyone knowing.' "

While acknowledging that an individual can legitimately take account of an injustice in dealing with the system, theologian Farley did not accept the simplified principle that "the system owes me this and I can do anything I want in order to get it." Other considerations enter in: how unfair, why unfair, whether a matter of opinion, whether greater harm will come from trying to set accounts straight. "You cannot judge the good of one person in isolation from other persons. Each of us exists in relation to others." This, she admitted, is a matter of individual judgment, but a judgment that should weigh more than one person's stakes.

Father Kenny urged "sensitivity to the moral implications of what all of us *tolerate* as well as *do*." Liberation theologian Snyder issued a challenge whenever anyone decides to "beat the system." The decision brings on a social responsibility: to work toward changing the system to make it more just, more fair. Otherwise, it is not an "adequate moral decision."

6

Buyer Beware

"Failure to inform prospective buyers is outright fraud."

"Principle of 'buyer beware' should apply. Prospective buyer should know enough to check things out. If seller told 'all,' he would never sell."

In buying and selling, the customer may always be right and still have no rights, as in a story told by New York's conscientious district attorney, Robert M. Morgenthau. It concerns a little boy who came home confused after the teacher talked about *ethics*.

"I didn't understand what the teacher was talking about," the boy reported. "What is ethics?"

"It's this way," said the father who was co-owner of a store. "A customer buys something and hands me $20. But when I get to the cash register, I notice he's handed me not one, but two $20 bills.

"Ethics is: Do I tell my partner?"

Since most people are customers most of the time, sympathies are with the buyer, not the seller. The consumer movement rose out of the smoldering resentment of buyers who had to beware and customers who felt cheated. One summer day in Washington, consumer advocate Ralph Nader described to me what gives him his "drive"—"a very strong sense of what is unjust." What buyers want is a fair deal from sellers.

53

In terms of everyday morality, a priest in the Passionist Order complained in epigram about Christians in business who cut Monday off from Sunday:

On Sunday the Bible is their ledger.
On Monday the ledger is their bible.

In surveying churchgoers, *Buyer Beware* situations evoked strong emotions, expressed in words like "terrible" and "disgusting." Others expressed weary acceptance of selling practices that call for buyer alertness. By contrast, Father Curran's notion of "enlightened self-interest" argued for seller honesty, since in business the argument is made that "honesty is the best policy." The worst advertisement is a dissatisfied customer. He or she will not only never come back, but also complain to friends. The best advertisement is a satisfied customer

A salesman knows a new line of products is continually breaking down. When asked about maintenance costs, he says the product has an outstanding record.

Among the emphatic answers:
"He's a liar and should quit a job where he can't be honest."
"He lies. Wrong!"
"It is dishonest to say that a product has an outstanding record when you know that it is always breaking down. That is a lie."
"He is obviously lying and besides everything else, he has to live with the fact that he can't be successful unless he 'pads the truth.' "
"The salesman is in serious error."
The place of truth in selling was discussed by those who said:
"He should tell the truth. Sometimes people are willing to chance a poor product if it is inexpensive. So he still might sell it. If he lies and sells the product and it is poor, he has lost that customer forever. His long-range loss is greater than the present sales loss."
"If a salesman knows the product isn't good, it seems to me he has a moral obligation to warn the buyer. It is being less than honest

54

when he withholds information the buyer needs to make an intelligent decision."

A customer likes a suit (or dress) and asks the salesperson if it fits properly. Though it does not, the salesperson says it fits because the proper size is no longer in stock.

It won't work, it won't work, it won't work. That was the reaction repeatedly, in effect reminding the salesperson of "enlightened self-interest":

"If it didn't look right, the salesperson should not say that it does. It would really hurt the business if the suit didn't fit and the buyer was asked where it was purchased."

"Liar—and the customer will *know* it!"

"This is a fairly common practice which hurts the customer and, I believe, the store. I, for sure, would never shop there again and would be hard pressed to live with myself if I were the salesperson."

"The salesperson should realize that eventually someone will tell the customer that it doesn't fit properly and the store will develop a bad reputation."

"This is wrong in my opinion. They will lose business in the long run."

"Wrong—and stupid. I never return to (or buy at) a place that operates like that."

Among the few who did not fault the salesperson, this was a typical line of reasoning: "If a customer likes a suit or dress, he thinks it fits properly in the first place and in asking a salesperson is only looking for reinforcement of his opinion. Only the customer knows if a garment fits the way he wants to have it fit and feel. He is free to buy or not to buy. The salesperson does nothing wrong if the customer likes the garment and he agrees with the customer."

A store owner announces a sale with a reduction of 20%. Actually, everything is marked higher than usual, then reduced 20% to the usual price.

Consumer outrage came through: "Sounds familiar—really makes me angry—I definitely think it's wrong."

"I feel a lot of the stores do this now and I think it's terrible."

"Standard procedure—but it is disgusting to experience this type of action."

"This, in my opinion, is very wrong, though I'm sure it is accepted as standard business procedure."

"I feel the owner is degrading himself."

"Even unsophisticated consumers would be aware of this. The store owner is a *fool* (besides a liar)!"

The few without outrage echoed the comment that this is the game of merchandising. "Nothing actually wrong with it. Most advertising is somewhat ambiguous. The store owner knows he can fool some of the people some of the time, but not all of the people all of the time. An intelligent shopper knows the merchandise and the store. He will only spend his money if he wants to."

If waiters and waitresses are expected to push the most expensive items on the menu, should they do so?

Apparently because the maneuver does not hoodwink customers and leaves their choice intact, this practice was taken in stride: "The customer still has the freedom to make his own choice." . . . "If they do, it's up to the customer to decide." . . . "No one is forced to order the most expensive items." . . . "People can decide for themselves." . . . "I don't like it, but it doesn't influence my decision."

Frequently, a condition was attached to this practice: that the items be worth the money: "If they feel they are worth the money asked." . . . "If they are indeed good and well-prepared." . . . "If they really believe the items are exceptional." . . . "Not unless they feel it is the best dish offered."

Comes another day and buyers become sellers, particularly of their cars and homes. Such as:

A couple is selling their home, which floods three or four times a year when it rains hard. Should they tell prospective buyers?

A number of people frankly admitted, as one respondent did, that it's a "hard question," adding: "Yes, you should tell the buyer about the flooding. But who would buy it? Doesn't the buyer have the responsibility of checking all that out?"

Others responded along similar lines: "If the prospective buyer asks, he should be told. I'm not sure if I would volunteer the information. I might—not sure." . . . "The seller should—but won't." . . . "Yes, you should. However, if it was my house and circumstances dictated a quick and profitable sale, I suppose I would downplay the leaks or maybe I wouldn't say anything at all." . . . "They should be told. However, if I was selling my home, I probably wouldn't mention anything unless I was specifically asked."

One homeowner spoke from personal experience in saying that the prospective buyer should be told. "This is a clear-cut decision. The buyers should be informed of anything that could affect them in such a drastic way. I lived in an area which flooded frequently. The homes were near a brook which frequently became swollen with heavy rain. The people in the area experienced tremendous hardship, both emotionally and financially."

Only a few saw no problem here, invoking the principle of *caveat emptor*. One respondent went so far as to say that "the only reason to tell would be if the flood could kill somebody."

Such situations are complicated when the buyer does check out information on the house and is told nothing is wrong:

A home buyer is assured by a roofer that the roof of a home he is buying is OK. But the owner knows the roof leaks. Should he tell the buyer?

"Yes. The buyer has the right to know exactly what he is getting and it is the owner's obligation to be honest."

"Yes. A leaky roof is serious! Why hasn't the owner told the roofer?"

"The owner should tell the prospective buyer the roof leaks and offer to fix it or adjust the price."

"Yes and negotiate to have it fixed, perhaps with those costs added to the buyer's price. The owner and buyer should find a compatible solution."

Some of those who agreed this should be done admitted, however, that "many would not tell."

Those who argued that the owner did not have to tell the buyer placed the burden on the roofer. As one New Jerseyan commented: "It's the roofer's responsibility."

In *Buyer Beware* situations, lay people and moral theologians walked side by side. Theologian Farley called truth-telling the "most important principle at stake"; the other theologians were as emphatic in rejecting a direct lie as a means toward the end of making a sale. Father McNulty viewed sellers "as making a kind of contract with the buyer that it is a legitimate sale, as owing it to the public that they're not lying."

In the case of waiters and waitresses pushing the most expensive items, the problem is not the action, but, as Father McNulty noted, the question, *Is the more expensive item worth the greater expense?* Otherwise, a legitimate form of salesmanship is involved when the seller tries to point buyer in a particular direction. The seller urges, the buyer decides.

Theologian Milhaven of Brown University stressed that *caveat emptor* is not a moral principle. Father Curran cited the moral principle that "a seller must reveal substantial defects." Accidental defects only should be revealed if asked about them; but here, too, the defects should be taken into account in setting the price. Father Curran then adds a complication: What is substantial? This is open to different interpretations, leaving the situation open to "legitimate diversity."

Going beyond individual situations, Father Curran stressed the "need for basic honesty in society": "When people stop taking that responsibility seriously, then the whole social fabric is endangered." He pointed out a corollary to the Golden Rule: "If you're going to give yourself permission to do something, then you must give everyone else the right to do it." Then, others would do unto you as you have done unto them.

7

Brother's Keeper

"No. It is not moral to work for the cigarette industry."

"I don't see any more immorality in participating in the tobacco industry than I find in working for a brewery or an auto manufacturer."

For what Henry Durham did, he faced the following:

Fellow employees called him a turncoat.

"Kill Durham" signs appeared on the bulletin board at the plant where he worked.

Lifelong friends refused to speak to him or his family.

Federal marshals had to move into his home for two months in order to protect him.

What Henry Durham did was to speak out against mismanagement, false documentation, and waste at a large defense plant where he was production-control supervisor. After trying for two years to get top company officials to listen, he quit his job, took his charges to the press, and testified before a Senate committee. The resulting government investigation exposed a cost overrun of $2 billion.

Henry Durham was acting on behalf of the taxpayers who foot the bill for defense spending. Doing his job at the expense of others—amorphous tax-paying others—was more than he could take. He "blew the whistle."

In the realm of looking out for others, the Golden Rule twists and turns in many directions in everyday living. Sometimes, action to expose; sometimes, inaction in order to oppose. Sometimes, helping others to endure; sometimes, restraining others from acting. Sometimes to cover up, sometimes to reveal. Sometimes to stand by, sometimes to step in. Always, the central question: What does it mean in daily life to be "my brother's keeper"?

In view of repeated government findings that cigarette smoking is dangerous to health, is it moral to work in or for the cigarette industry? Is it moral to buy shares of stock in the cigarette industry and collect dividends on their profits?

While few people thought working for a cigarette company wrong, buying stocks was frequently another matter. One candid answer summarized the paradox: "I find this a difficult question. The smoker has the choice of whether to buy cigarettes or not. Therefore, I feel morally you can work for a cigarette company. While there probably shouldn't be any distinction, I believe it is wrong to buy shares and collect dividends on their profits. Perhaps this is illogical thinking."

Along similar lines: "I don't believe it is immoral to work in or for the tobacco industry, but I would not buy stocks in the industry. I don't want to profit (perhaps) at the expense of the health of others. I personally believe smoking is harmful, but so are dozens of other things, such as liquor, cars, etc." . . . "It is moral to do either, but I would think twice before I bought such stock." . . . "If it's the only thing available, work—but don't buy stock."

Others rejected the idea that a moral question is involved, repeatedly citing the free choice to smoke or not to smoke:

"Like drinking, smoking is a matter of free choice. It is not a moral issue unless someone endangers his or her health knowingly."

"There are many things in life that are dangerous. Car accidents kill as many as or more than cigarettes."

"Cigarette smoking is potentially dangerous, but there is still some room for doubt. Many people have smoked all their lives

60

without developing health problems. Therefore, I don't think it's a moral issue."

"Everyone has the right to smoke or not to smoke."

"Individuals who smoke make a free choice to ruin or kill their bodies. If God gives us the freedom to commit sins, how are we justified in taking away a person's freedom to choose to smoke? I think the company fulfills its obligation to morality by stating on the package that smoking is hazardous to your health."

"Since, in my opinion, this is not a moral issue, I probably would work in the industry. Eating certain foods is dangerous to health. Does that mean I also shouldn't work on a vegetable or livestock farm or in a grocery store where all of the above are sold?"

The situation is touchy for those who themselves smoke, as one Lutheran noted: "I have a difficult time answering this question mainly because I smoke at times. If working for the company is immoral, then my smoking is also immoral. Or is it?"

A non-smoking wife was "glad" she was not in the situation because she would not be "happy" working for a tobacco company and "definitely" would not buy tobacco stocks. "But then again I'm not happy with my husband's pipe smoking, but I'm not leaving him."

A New Jerseyan commented that for anyone who is against smoking it would be "contradictory" to work for a tobacco company, then added: "I do not smoke, therefore I would not buy shares of stock in the tobacco industry."

A supervisor is required to maintain a production line turning out unsafe products. He learns that his predecessor was fired for bringing this up and he knows production will continue with or without him.

Not only *don't do it*, but try to remedy the situation—that was the gist of most answers.

First of all, the supervisor was advised that "he has a moral obligation to speak up and, if necessary, to carry it further." He "needs to examine his moral concern for the safety of others, even if it means the loss of his job."

Others answered: "I don't mean to sound holier than thou, but

61

I just couldn't do it—at the risk of losing my job." . . . "If the supervisor continued to maintain production, he would be morally wrong." . . . "He should not continue if he doesn't want to be a part of something that is unsafe for others." . . . "Unless his family would die of starvation, he should leave the situation (unless there is some possibility that by staying he could correct it)." . . . "If the 'unsafe' factor was real (not a far-fetched possibility by over-zealous consumer watchdogs), definitely I'd take action."

Repeatedly, going outside the company was suggested, indicating that many Christians include the consumer movement, Naderism, and "whistle blowing" in their everyday morality. "He should report unsafe products to Ralph Nader or someone like that." . . . "Report to government bureau responsible for safety standards, withholding your name." . . . "Appeal to the proper authorities outside the company." . . . "Hopefully, I could voice the problem somehow—the union or public opinion, such as a newspaper." . . . "If the product is a real threat to life, he should inform the media." . . . "If speaking to the company wouldn't help, I would write to someone who could stop this practice."

X's colleague regularly receives money under the table from a supplier. There is nothing wrong with the supplies in quality or price. Should X expose the colleague?

The responses ranged from "it's not my business" to "let those in charge know but withhold name."

Reasons for not exposing the colleague centered on not becoming "another person's conscience," a viewpoint expressed in various ways: "I would consider it wrong, but I would not impose my beliefs on him. I would let him know my feelings." . . . "Depends on weighing the situation, how common the practice is, if it is known and expected. I'd try to dialogue with him on his perception of what he is about." . . . "I would try to convince the colleague to stop accepting the money. If he didn't, I probably wouldn't report him." . . . "I would speak to the colleague as subtly as possible, noting it is wrong and he is compromising his position." . . . "I would try to convince the colleague to stop accepting the money. If he didn't, I probably wouldn't report him."

On the other hand, if trying to convince him didn't succeed, exposure was suggested by some. One condition emerged: not to expose out of jealously, but out of "true moral instinct."

When two circumstances were added to the situation, one produced little change in reactions, the other sealed a decision to expose. When the supposition was added that the "materials are inferior," exposure dominated the reactions: "If the materials are inferior, the position is clear. The corruption should be exposed." . . . "Confront the colleague and expose him if it is not stopped." . . . "Probably would take action leading to exposure." . . . "Since this implies that someone somewhere is definitely being cheated, most certainly expose, yes." . . . "If the inferiority of the supplies is being concealed by making additional payments, I would definitely expose the people involved, unless extenuating circumstances were involved. Then I would simply expose the inferiority of the supplies."

If the colleague is being underpaid, this was viewed as another issue which did not affect the decision to expose or not to expose. For the most part, people responding to the situation stuck to their guns: "Another injustice, *but* another issue." . . . "Shouldn't matter." . . . "No reason to gyp your employer." . . . "Wouldn't change my opinion if I thought a moral wrong was involved."

A colleague at work asks you to help conceal an extra-marital affair by phoning messages to his or her partner.

Time and again, any friend who asked for such a "favor" was, in effect, told: *That's going too far. You have no right or fair claim in involving me.* Rejection was emphatic: "No way!" . . . "Absolutely not." . . . "No way. His problem." . . . "No. Let him cheat on his own." . . . "No one of any intelligence would get involved in this mess! An absolute no." . . . "No one should meddle in marital matters." . . . "I would not help to deceive a partner." . . . "Absolutely not. I would never do it!"

"When a partner feels the need to have an extra-marital affair," an Illinois Catholic commented, "there is something very basic missing in the marriage and it will never again be regained."

In going further with the situation, the circumstances were stacked to see whether conscientious Christians would bend for the sake of the marriage and children.

Suppose a close friend asks you to help conceal an extra-marital affair and you know that his marriage goes on for the sake of the children only. You know the partner makes life miserable for your friend and that the partner is highly neurotic and easily upset.

Help, yes. Deception, no.

"Sorry, I might try to help in other ways."

"I would suggest my friend seek professional help and counseling. If the marriage is being saved for the sake of the children, it is more than likely the children already know something is wrong!"

"Advise counseling of some sort. Many times good comes from this."

"I would not cooperate, but would offer a sympathetic ear and urge counseling for both. The friend needs help in correcting the situation, not compounding it."

"I would try to direct her in the right channels where all would benefit. I would definitely pray."

In making up their minds not to help in the deception, a number of people commented that the children don't benefit by the situation at all: "I would still say no. The children would probably be better off if the marriage broke up." . . . "The children will suffer just as much, if not more, during this affair.". . ."Children do not profit from living with two adults who are dishonest with each other and pretend to love each other. They would be better off in the end to be with one parent who is able to build a new relationship with a loving partner. Living with a 'highly neurotic' individual is not good for children or mate, and catering to a neurotic is not helping him or her."

The argument was advanced with a discussion of what friendship involves: "The friend pursues his affair for his own reasons.

You should not aid him. If friendship is based on whether you help him or not, then it is not worth it. One affair leads to another. There would be no end to your involvement—and legal complications, too!"

A friend is planning an abortion for convenience and asks you to come along for psychological support. What would you say or do?

If a friend wants psychological support for an abortion, then for many Catholics morality and friendship are on a collision course. Repeatedly, rejection of psychological support seemed linked to strong feelings against abortion. "Absolutely reprehensible," said one person. "There can be no excuse for murder." Another said: "If someone (a friend, but not real close) were planning an abortion for convenience, I would not call that person my friend anymore."

This point of view was spelled out in various ways: "I would tell her my views on abortion. I am against it. I would counsel her to think of giving the baby up for adoption if she were single. Beyond that, I would do nothing. I would not accompany her. I would expect any *friend* to understand my feelings." ... "No! I would do everything in my power to persuade her not to do it. Would under no circumstances accompany her." ... "If I hadn't been able to convince her that abortion is murder by the time she was actually going in for the abortion, I would be no help in psychological support."

However, others who opposed abortion saw no conflict in offering such psychological support. They would make known their opposition to abortion, condemning the sin rather than the sinner, as one person said: A typical reasoning process ran this way: "This is a sticky one. I don't believe in abortion and yet if someone else has made the decision and is my friend, I would go along for psychological support if their decision was final. I don't think it would be right for me to lay my own guilt trip onto somebody else."

Since Monday morality takes place "on the spot," the responses to the above questions probably came close to the way individual Christians would react. They were asked to respond—unprepared—to situations from everyday living. No time for reflection, no set of moral rules and regulations were handed out, no promise of a definitive ruling on right and wrong. That is the way life is lived: on the run—or at least in motion. The time for ethical reflection usually comes later.

Moral theologians supply that reflection, as individual Christians can supply it for themselves after a decision or action. While reflection does not help past decision-making, it does help with present and future decisions. It helps tune you into your views of right and wrong and the values involved. It spotlights commitments and focuses on priorities, on what really counts in making everyday moral decisions.

In the realm of being your "brother's keeper," the searchlight of the moralist moves in various directions and in the end the individual is left holding his or her own searchlight, more knowledgeable and more alert, but without a standardized answer. Consider various comments by moral theologians on working for a cigarette company:

McNULTY: "The cigarette situation is a relatively new one. Doctors for whom I have a lot of respect are very strong on this. One surgeon is absolutely sure that cigarette smoking is terribly harmful. I think we in the pulpit should speak out more on the issue. You're not going to make a hit with smokers, but you're really doing them a favor. You're encouraging them to stop smoking and giving them some backing on doing so by reminding them of their obligation to take care of their lives.

"If people are already working in the cigarette industry, they are in a real bind because they got into it and made money in it before they knew the great harm. So I would be tolerant of what they're doing out of necessity. But I think a person would have to think over getting into it now or buying cigarette stocks.

"On the other side, some medical opinion holds that maybe cigarette smoking isn't that harmful, so I guess the person will have to make up his or her mind on whom to listen to. Personally, since I don't smoke and have no cigarette stocks, I am certainly inclined to believe the doctors. Very significant for me is the large number of doctors who have quit smoking."

CURRAN: "One person says, 'I think smoking is wrong and I want no part of it.' Obviously that is making a personal witness. The other viewpoint is: 'I've got to respect other people. They are over 21, they can read the warnings, and they still want to smoke. Therefore, I may be respecting the rights and even the abilities of other people.' If everyone pulled out of what he personally thinks is wrong, you would have difficulty living in a pluralistic society."

Father Curran was more directive when pressed. Suppose someone who strongly opposed smoking as harmful to others needed a job and was offered a good one by a cigarette company. The job would enable his family to hold on to its standard of living.

"This obviously is something you must work through," he replied. "It's the old problem that untried virtue is really not virtue at all. If you were truly convinced beforehand about smoking, then I really think you've got to be true to yourself, to your own commitments. If one truly made those commitments and they are that important, then I think you say *no*."

Theologian Farley focused on the principle of *material cooperation*—"very helpful and very hard to apply." While not agreeing that an action is right, not wanting the action and not doing anything wrong, in some way the individual's material cooperation allows it to go on. (In formal cooperation, you participate in an evil action and also share its intention.) The individual has to wrestle with various questions on whether to work for a cigarette company or on that production line with unsafe products.

Am I called upon to perform immoral actions (such as lying)?

How great and how certain will be the harm?

What will be the effect of my refusal to cooperate?

Will it change the situation?

What will be the effect on me and my family?

Different answers for different individuals. But you do have to ask and answer these questions, theologian Farley emphasized. "If it won't make any difference if I cease to cooperate and if the evil that has been perpetrated is not as great as the evil if I lose my job, then I could justify continuing to cooperate." As a protection against taking the easy way out, there is theologian Snyder's emphasis on having a reference group—concerned others with whom to dialogue on moral and religious concerns.

The notion itself of *brother's keeper* was clarified. "You're not obliged in business to be your brother's keeper." (McNulty) "Being

67

your brother's judge has less priority than positive helping as a brother's keeper. Where people would be hurt, whistle blowing is justified, but not necessarily called for when the only thing happening is your colleague's wrong actions." (Farley)

Dr. Snyder placed *brother's keeper* within the framework of social responsibility. He suggested leaking information on the product to outside authorities "so you are not personally exposed." He would feel morally justified in lying if confronted by management and asked if he leaked such information. "I would justify the lie on the basis that I was not simply preserving my job but trying to change the situation that is hurting a number of people. For example, if I knew that a particular car model were defective, I would bear a responsibility to make that information available in a form that can actually change its production—not just in a form that lets me appear as a moral martyr. Telling the truth and admitting I leaked the information might end up in my feeling morally superior, but if it doesn't change the car's production, then I have failed to correct the situation."

Lying to conceal a colleague's extra-marital affair was another matter. That kind of helping was rejected by Theologian Farley ("You yourself are asked to do something which you perceive to be evil, which is to tell a lie"), by Father Curran ("No, I would not lie to conceal"), and by Father McNulty ("You would be doing a friend a disservice and certainly being unfair to the partner"). In line with his social-responsibility approach, Dr. Snyder rejected the "casual request" to lie, but could visualize helping with a lie if the colleague were willing to enter a serious discussion and look into the marital problem. A simple cover-up was not acceptable, but he did leave open the possibility of holding off a partner's suspicion as a prelude to taking on the responsibility of becoming involved constructively in the marital problem. Then the action becomes a matter of carrying a heavier moral burden, rather than doing a friend a favor by lying.

Offering psychological support in the case of abortion went against the moral position of the Catholic moral theologians. Responding as an opponent of abortion who said that "after three weeks you have truly human life," Father Curran would set forth his opposition and would not provide psychological support. Father

McCormick would refuse to go along, saying, "I'm sorry." If there were any doubt why, he would explain his opposition to abortion.

"To accompany a woman having an abortion would be against my conscience," Father Kenny said. "It's not in keeping with my respect for life." But he would make himself available afterwards to help if problems developed, and he would "respect a person's right to make the decision."

Father McNulty also would offer support afterwards, but he "could never go along for psychological support." He would "try to be tolerant of the person's decision, but feel a real obligation to speak for the life of that unborn child," talking "loud and long" about it. Once done, he "would show plenty of mercy and compassion and understanding." By not going along, he would not be supportive of the action; afterwards, he could be "supportive of the person."

Theologian Farley said she saw both sides of the situation. Opponents of abortion would see accompanying someone as "going along with something they thought was wrong"; conversely, the woman undergoing the abortion "may fall apart and need you to be there." The decision to accompany or not comes down to "your perception of the woman's needs and the possible larger consequences of your action (for example, whether your presence at an abortion clinic would be misunderstood)."

Here are "important questions" raised by Dr. Farley: "What does it mean to say this is an abortion of 'convenience'? What, in fact, are the reasons for your friend's choice? Is it important for her that you oppose the choice in every way? Or ought you to respond affirmatively to her in spite of her choice? Does your judgment regarding her choice have to be the sole determinant of your action in her regard? What really is best for her and for others with whom she is in relation?"

That is where the theologians left the listener in commenting on being your *brother's keeper*. It's not necessarily yours to judge, but to help. But it's not yours to help with actions violating your view of right and wrong, unless you feel justified for the sake of a greater good.

8

"Amending" the Sixth Commandment

"Wrong. Their love for each other cannot be very strong if they can't solve the financial problem any other way than by living together."

"More power to them."

Writers about sex invariably give in to temptation—the temptation to circle the subject by citing chapter, verse, example, and advice and by quoting Augustine and Aquinas, Freud and Havelock Ellis, as well as Kinsey and Masters and Johnson.

For Monday morality, a Methodist wife and mother from a small New England town moved expeditiously into the basic issue: "My husband and I have had sexual intercourse with each other and no one else," she responded along with 60,000 to a *McCall's* magazine survey. "Neither of us had sex with someone else before we were married, and we waited until we were married to have intercourse. This a bond we have only with each other, and over our 26 years of married life no two times have been exactly the same."

That essentially is the issue of sex confronting Christians in everyday living. What about sex between two people who are not married to each other? Non-marital, pre-marital, extra-marital. The issue boils down to individual "amendments" to the traditional restrictions of the Sixth Commandment—that one out of ten commandments which seems to bestride Christianity like a Colossus.

Even when "amendments" to the Sixth are out of the question for churchgoing Christians, changes may come into their lives via children, such as a familiar situation for parents of young adults:

The Smiths have a son (or daughter) at college who returns home with a steady date. They want to spend the weekend together in the same room.

The overwhelming reaction was that *this is going too far.* What sons and daughters do elsewhere in violation of the traditional sexual ethic was one thing, but "not in my house," as one New Jerseyan commented. A number of answers noted that letting this happen implied approval and stressed that children should not flaunt defiance of their parents' standards: "This is against my morals and my child would have to abide with my wishes in my house." . . . "Wrong. Allowing would be approving." . . . "Smiths should not compromise their principles in their own home to accommodate child." . . . "Wrong. Rules of your house should be respected by young people." . . . "What they do at college, you cannot control, but you can control what happens in your own home, especially with younger children in the home." . . . "You can make the rules in your own home. You have no control away from home. But don't wait until the last minute and be unpleasant." . . . "If the parents don't approve, I feel they have a right to say no. If the son/daughter feels this decision violates his/her rights, he/she has a right to stay elsewhere."

Many stuck to this position even when their own children were not involved, as in the case where an unmarried couple invited for the weekend expect to share the same room: "This is against my standards—no way!" . . . "I would explain my views and ask that they consider my moral position for just this weekend." . . . "They wouldn't be invited again." . . . "I'd provide separate facilities."

Others were ready to accept "amendments" to the Sixth Commandment made by others, arguing that they "are old enough to decide what is right for them." Some of the same people who would say no to their own children explained that they accepted the practice when it involves two "consenting adults," though they do not personally approve. As long as no "scandal" were involved

71

for younger children in the house, they were ready to let unmarried weekend guests share the same room:

"This should be worked out ahead of time. I see nothing wrong with it if no one objects."

"OK, with two consenting adults and no younger children in the house."

"This arrangement would not offend me, if it did not cause any 'explanation' problems with my children."

"They should have thought it out before issuing the invitation. Yes, if it is their way of life."

"Wrong, but I would permit it if I had no children in the house."

"Right—or don't invite them."

"If the hosts are aware of and accepting of the relationship, there is no problem in sharing a room. If the hosts aren't accepting of the relationship, don't invite the couple together."

"It would depend on how well I know the couple and their families. Normally, I would say yes."

Two responses which typified differing reactions to changing sexual mores were:

"Wrong. Our culture seems to be changing more and more. Unmarried couples are living together. My views on this have not changed. My experience is that those couples end up having problems, many of which are not solved because they have no binding relationship. I cannot encourage this practice."

"In this day and time, I think it would be all right if that is how the hosts had it planned. Otherwise, the guests should go by the wishes of their hosts."

John and Mary are engaged, but can't afford to marry until he graduates from law school. The only way he can afford to stay in school is for them to move in together.

Against a background of condemnation, "amendments" showed signs of acceptance. First, the condemnation:

"Wrong. There is such a thing as self-control."

"If they can afford to live together, they can afford to get married."

"Wrong. I don't see how getting through school would depend on living together. Get a job!"

"No. Poor excuse!"

"Mary" was warned that she would pay the price. "In most cases, the female is the one most "hurt." . . . "If they live together and the relationship is really not together, she might be on the losing end because he might leave after getting through school, since he has already had the benefits of married life."

Others, while rejecting the notion of living together for themselves, read and accept signs of the times: "A few years ago, I'd say wrong, but now with so many marriages breaking up so soon, I'd be more tolerant. Can't see myself doing it, however." . . . "They are of age. You have no say. If they want to do so, they will. It is no longer frowned upon socially."

Among those accepting the situation, a characteristic response was: "No problem. The real marriage is the commitment between the two people."

A Catholic husband who does not believe in divorce persists in an unhappy marriage. He develops a close platonic friendship with a divorced woman who has no desire to remarry. After two years of friendship, she suggests having sexual relations from time to time.

This was summarized as trying to "have your cake and eat it, too." Most advised the husband to stop "trying to go both ways." . . . "Either he should not persist in the unhappy marriage or he surely should end the relationship while still in the marriage."

Other answers echoed this viewpoint: "This is an adulterous situation. He cannot have both no divorce and this relationship." . . . "The relationship is no longer platonic and is a betrayal of marriage vows. Either get a divorce or sever the relationship. Adultery is never right." . . . "His religious teaching shines through in one area, but is contradicted in another. He needs counseling. He needs an opportunity to express his feelings to someone who can help. To lead a double life is wrong. He should give up one or the other woman. He isn't being fair to either of them. The second woman certainly has no feeling for anyone but herself. She also needs help."

The argument was fortified by citing consequences: "He's probably headed for trouble in that 'having sex from time to time' is hardly a permanent arrangement. It's like eating half a piece of a scrumptious chocolate cake. I doubt they'd leave the second half. They had best discuss where things are headed." . . . "This is sad because it is a situation where the woman will be a disappointed person after the urges for sex give way to bitterness." . . . "It seems the strain of the situation might either end their friendship or his marriage. (Perhaps that would be for the better.) However, I don't think they could live peacefully with this arrangement for long."

The minority view was represented by this comment: "Right. It's a compromise and a trade-off for mental health—unless guilt feelings would be overpowering."

Within marriage, sex and the married Catholic involves the problem of the pill (or any contraceptive method other than the widely-rejected rhythm). While surveys show that most Catholics have made up their minds in favor of birth control, individual responses reveal different paths of thought.

John and Mary have three children—ages 6 to 12—and they are falling behind in their bills. They decide to have no more children so that Mary can go to work. They decide to use the pill.

The few who called this wrong did not elaborate. The majority who approved the pill went in two directions:
1. Couples have the right to make up their own minds.
2. Children will suffer if unwanted.

The first group reasoned: "The couple must decide according to their own conscience." . . . "If using the pill is against a moral sanction which they feel is integral to their lives, they should not use the pill. If not, go ahead." . . . "It's their decision and nothing was forced on them." . . . "Right. Falling further into debt and becoming dependent on welfare, etc., while having more children does not seem to me what Christ would ask of them." . . . "Right, if Mary has explored all types of contraception and decides the pill is the right choice for her."

The second group reasoned: "Far better than to have an unwanted child whom they can't support. All the children would suffer." . . . "It's perfectly fine. If a person or persons know that they cannot afford the children they have, why bring others into the world to be deprived of everything." . . . "This is correct as all will suffer and perhaps hurt them in many other ways—fights between parents, hence destroying home life."

When the situation was altered to give as a reason for using the pill "more freedom to enjoy themselves," the couple was accused of being selfish. A typical reaction: "In this case, the couple is being selfish. If you can afford children, you should at least have one!"

"Selfishness" was also cited as justification for using the pill: "If they are looking for freedom, another child will make them unhappy. The child will suffer in the long run. Better to use the pill than have a child who will be mistreated." . . . "It is up to them and it is probably for the welfare of their children. If they want to be free and enjoy life, children would only get in the way and everyone would be unhappy." . . . "Better than to be bad parents."

In the view of moral theologians (as well as sociologists) birth control appears to be "for many persons a non-problem" (according to theologian Farley) or "a moral issue that Catholics have solved" (according to theologian Curran). Father McNulty tries to bridge the gap between official Church teaching and the freedom most Catholics feel to practice birth control. He noted the "tension that must be balanced." *John* and *Mary* must make their decison to use the pill "with the full knowledge that the Catholic Church teaches that contraception is sinful and they shouldn't do it, but the Church also teaches, and has always taught, freedom of conscience."

While the Catholic Church has had little success in getting its moral theologians to line up in orderly fashion behind the official teaching on birth control, debate on sex outside marriage thus far has been limited. The accepted norm is that sexual intercourse should be marital. In ruling out non-marital, pre-marital, and extra-marital sex, Father McCormick has been empathic: "Since sexual intercourse and its proximate antecedents represent *total personal* exchange, they can be separated from total personal relationship (marriage) only by undermining their truly human, their expressive character—in short their significance." He labels sex outside marriage as "objectively, even if not consciously, an act of manipulation."

Father Curran, who is widely respected for his wisdom as well as his courage as a moral theologian, has offered these considerations:

"Sex expresses a personal relationship: it does not create one.

Then the theoretical question comes: how strong a personal relationship must there be?"

Father Curran answered his own question: "One could argue then that the fullest of personal relationships is a total commitment and a permanent giving of one person to another. One might say that every sexual relationship doesn't invove that kind of personal relationship. I would argue that you should tend toward it.

"My other argument is one that I don't think I see enough of in most of the contemporary literature. It comes from the twofold aspect of human limitation and human sinfulness. Namely, that some kind of regulation of human sexuality is necessary because of the dangers and problems that can arise and have arisen in the past."

Notwithstanding, does that make *all* sex outside marriage immoral? Or can there be exceptions which are moral? Theologian Curran, in effect, says theoretically *yes*, but practically speaking *no*. Theologian Farley says there is a strong possibility that exceptions can be justified.

CURRAN: "A very important value in society centers on marriage. Granted all the problems and difficulties of families these days, we have to try to protect marriage and the family. If you allow sex outside marriage, you are weakening the family. By allowing it even in one or two cases, you might open the door to allowing it in other cases. Though you could justify it in one or two cases, we should say no. It is like the policy in state parks when there is a drought and signs forbid all campfires. A boy scout could probably build a very careful fire and there would be no danger. But because of the common danger, no one can build a campfire."

FARLEY: "In the area of sexual relations, I would start with the norms of justice. Rather than focusing on the traditional question: What is the goal of the sexual organs? I would ask: What constitutes justice in relations between persons? This means that my fundamental ethical principle would not be that every sexual act must be open to procreation, but that every sexual act must meet and express the principle of respect for persons. It would follow, minimally, that sex should never be used to dominate, exploit, or objectify either women or men, and that violence is never justified in sexual relations. It would follow, maximally, that sex should foster and express the fullest form of human friendship—which ordinarily is hoped for in the relationship of marriage."

Theologian Farley indicates some dissatisfaction with the claim that "people do tend to exploit one another if they don't have a permanent commitment with one another when they have sex together." Such a claim should, she says, be based on empirical evidence, adding: "Without such evidence (which we do not have in any conclusive way—and may never have) the moral possibility of sex outside marriage remains open." As a specialist in Christian ethics with a growing reputation in both Protestant and Catholic circles, she emphasizes relationship, commitment, justice, respect, mutual fulfillment, personal dignity. This "doesn't necessarily without qualification restrict sexual activity only to marriage."

Whereas lay Christians answered emphatically in terms of do's and don'ts, moral theologians preferred to stress values, as in Father Kenny's description of how he would counsel someone on sex (drawing on training as a moral theologian and on more than 20 years of pastoral experience):

"I don't feel that as a priest or confessor or moral leader my job is to say that this is right or this wrong. All I'm doing then is fortifying the simple solutions: if you follow the rules of the game, everything will be OK. Rather, I'd start by helping a person dig into the deeper meaning of marriage. Is sex bad beforehand because you don't have a legal ceremony, and is it OK tomorrow after you have one? That's the kind of logic that justifies a legally married man coming home drunk and virtually raping his wife. After all, he's got a marriage certificate. No, that's not the meaning, the finality of marriage. The meaning and beauty of marriage is centered in a total self-giving that has evolved to the point where you're ready to express it fully."

In terms of upholding your sexual norms with your own children, the moral theologians readily agreed that parents should stand up for them in the face of college-age children wanting to spend the night with a friend under the parental roof. In the case of adult guests, respecting their freedom was not seen as a compromise. And in the case of extra-marital sex, the theologians emphasized the obligation of fidelity: "The principle of not harming another and the principle of promise-keeping rule out extra-marital sex." (Farley) "Calculated unfaithfulness to a spouse destroys the total giving, the total communication that marriage requires." (Kenny)

What remained is the question of who decides whether a relationship is deep enough to justify sex without benefit of clergy? A reference to the community in dialogue on morality is necessary. Common practice and collective judgment all deserve a hearing, as does their particular church authority for all Christians. But, as one theologian noted, no theologian is going to "commit to hell" anyone engaged in sex outside marriage. Rules are rules, but in the last analysis—as one lay person pointed out—"each person has to answer to God for his or her own acts."

9

Taxation with Misrepresentation

"Wrong. Padding income tax returns is illegal and it is cheating and lying."

"This is what you pay your accountant to do."

In New York, a businessman claimed income tax deductions for no less than 338 "business lunches" in a single year.

In Chicago, a 70-year-old grandfather received $10,000 a year in cash working for his son, the liquor store owner. But nothing declared, nothing officially earned. And no taxes.

In Hollywood, a part-time actor reported $2,700 income as a handyman instead of the $12,000 he actually earned in cash.

Back in Washington, when President Carter cited the businessman who could crowd so many business lunches into a single year, he complained that the $10,000 in "so-called business lunches" was "more than many American families make in all, and the average working American had to pay that guy's taxes for him."

When the *Chicago Sun-Times* worked with a civic group to uncover corruption, a local accountant reported that out of 700 local businesses he handled, all but four cheated on taxes. Eight of ten other local accountants were contacted and they offered one piece of tax advice: *cheat*.

In the world of taxation, income is not only under-reported and expenses over-reported. Income may not be reported at all. The federal General Accounting Office estimated that each year five million wage earners do not file tax returns, thereby avoiding $2 billion in taxes. (About half of the non-filers earned $5,000 or less; only four percent earned $20,000 or more.)

But that $2 billion national evasion is slight compared to the income generated by the sprawling "subterranean economy" of unreported income, particularly income earned by taxpayers who report only part of their income. Economics professor Peter M. Gutmann of the City University of New York has estimated total unreported income in the United States, combining the fruits of both legitimate and illegitimate activities. He estimates that it amounts to ten percent of the gross national product: $176 billion unreported in 1976, $195 billion in 1977, $220 billion in 1978.

While other experts regard his estimates as too high, no one doubts that many billions are involved and, in the process, millions of Americans. According to the Internal Revenue Service, the single biggest tax evasion is failure by individuals and corporations to report bank interest and stock dividends. Next come those who don't report all or part of income received in cash or even in checks.

Former IRS commissioner Sheldon Cohen has pointed out that evasion follows temptation and the temptation is greatest in "areas that handle large amounts of small cash payments, and even if checks are given, there's no record in many cases." Thus, he added, those most tempted are waiters, maids, doctors, small shopkeepers and businessmen, workmen, and independent craftsmen.

But whoever the taxpayer, the system is based on trust. There are too many taxpayers (almost 90 million) watched by too few in the IRS (about 25,000). In any year, only two million taxpayers are actually audited and while three out of four have to pay additional taxes, less than 2,000 are actually indicted for fraud (1,641 in 1977). The odds weigh heavily in favor of the taxpayer and depend mainly on his or her conscience, including those who believe in "taxation with misrepresentation."

At income tax time, X looks for ways to pad deductions and donations and invent expenses, then

**itemizes these fictitious claims to reduce the amount
of tax.**

There were those who saw such tactics in terms of the Ten
Commandments, those who saw them in terms of their attitude toward government and their responsibility to society, and those who
just worried about getting caught.

A typical representative of the Ten Commandments' reaction
stated: "This practice combines stealing and lying and is clearly
wrong. Futhermore, it is not really the government which is
gypped—it is the persons who honestly report their income and pay
their taxes. The government is going to exact so much in taxes, and
when cheaters defraud the IRS the government raises the levy and
we are all made to repay what the tax cheat held back." (Professor
Gutmann has even argued that taxes on unreported income in the
"subterranean economy" would practically erase the U.S. budget
deficit.)

Another answer was brief and specific: "Wrong. Violation of
the Commandments. It is stealing." Similarly: "In all honesty, I find
it hard to do because I have a guilt feeling about lying and then sign-
ing a statement saying everything I've said is true." . . . "Wrong. It's
cheating—making claims that cannot be substantiated." . . . "Cheating the government and lying are both wrong." . . . "Not only stealing from Uncle Sam, but also attributing donations to charitable
institutions when you do not donate is pretty low." There was even
an apocalyptic response: "An obvious sign of the sort of decay in
personal and civic virtue which appears at the close of all civiliza-
tions dying from within."

Those who saw taxes as part of their responsibility to society
joined in condemning misrepresentation: "X doesn't have a sense of
responsibility to the society in which he/she participates and is mo-
tivated by self-interest." . . . "This action would be wrong. Such an
individual would not be bearing a fair share of taxes. As a result, another party would end up paying more than a fair share of the
load." . . . "I guess the thing that bothers me the most is that most
people who have the knowledge and resources to do this have no
trouble affording their taxes."

Even some of those who were angry at government and at taxes opposed going too far to evade taxes: "It is not wrong to take advantage of legal loopholes to avoid taxes. However, it is unethical to fraudulently submit non-existent deductions." . . . "This is wrong, but it is difficult for me to really condemn anyone who rips off an institution of the size and character of the U.S. government." . . . "Wrong in a minor way. Government is destroying us by high taxes and spending. The individual must protect himself." . . . "Wrong. We should be fair and honest in this, too. But the pinch is great for the average working person. I think we should try to get legislation worked out to get greater fairness in the tax structure. There is something wrong when large corporations get off with tax shelters and the working man must pay and pay."

Other angry taxpayers used their anger to justify tax-evading tactics: "The government has such a high tax rate that I feel any means of reducing the burden is justifiable. The cost of living has risen so, it's difficult to feed a family, let alone support our politicians." . . . "There are instances in which one can find the government so 'crooked' that it could drive an individual to do this in order to meet rising costs, etc." . . . "OK. My personal opinion is that taxes are a monumental rip-off."

A Catholic mother of school children combined a number of grievances in responding: "I wish to point out that it is *my* money, not the government's, and this government has long ago exceeded any claims it might have to distributive collective justice regarding taxes. There are millionaires paying no income taxes. Furthermore, my tax money is used to fund Planned Parenthood and medicaid abortions, but my parochial-school children aren't good enough to get *their* share of the tax dollar for values-oriented education. To be crude, the hell with Uncle Sam!"

Those who worried primarily about the consequences of cheating commented: "No, only because I don't want to pay a fine if I got caught." . . . "No. I'm always afraid I would get caught." . . . "Not only is this wrong, but it is extremely stupid. One audit and the expenses can be compounded tremendously." . . . "Sooner or later, the taxpayer will get caught and pay for the mistake one way or another." . . . "It can only be said to be wrong if the taxpayer gets caught."

Taxpayer reports only some of the tips earned on the job in order to save on income taxes.

Most who said "wrong" did not elaborate, possibly because they regarded the issue as a matter of personal integrity. As stated by one Catholic: "You are guilty in the eyes of God and that's the only one we have to answer to."

Most of those justifying the practice argued that "it's done all the time" or that the money was needed: "With inflation, what can one do? Feel noble without shoes or not so bad with shoes?" . . . "Acceptable. The government takes enough in taxes for the middle people. We have no oil depletion or other tax loopholes, so we make up our own." . . . "If the income is really needed for living, it is right." . . . "Some feel justified because base pay is so low."

The tolerant view was epitomized in this response: "It's not all that bad. How much can a person's tips help the government? It might be dishonest, but one has to survive and scrap for what he can get. I wouldn't judge a person as bad and unrighteous because he did not report all his tips."

Businessmen received a similar set of mixed reactions, though not as much sympathy:

A businessman makes a few sales every month "off the books" in order to save on taxes and to keep up with the inflationary spiral of costs.

"A businessman, in his position, should feel more responsibility toward his government" was one view echoed by: "We are obliged to live within our income, small though it may be. Some people's jobs do not give them the 'chance' to earn 'off the books' and it is wrong for others who have the chance to do so." One wife noted that her husband "is in his own business and does not use this procedure."

On the other hand, "go ahead and do it" advice was accompanied by the complaint that the "middle class is unfairly taxed while the very rich have all the loopholes and the very poor don't pay taxes."

The view that "it all depends" was discussed in terms of the circumstances: "If the man is in desperate need of extra money and needs to support a family, then it can't be all that bad. No one is a saint. Just so long as the businessman doesn't do it too much and let it get out of hand." . . . "The degree of culpability would depend on whether or not he owned the business and to what his particular cost of living was due, such as sickness and medical bills or simply keeping up one's 'country club' standard of living."

Homeowners received even less sympathy in the following situation:

A homeowner facing property reassessment and higher real estate taxes does not report the new wing added to his house.

Aside from labeling evasion wrong, the homeowner was repeatedly advised that it won't work—"a new wing is hard to hide." In addition: "If everyone thought that way what kind of world would it be?" . . . "He is cheating. He should not add on if he cannot afford all the expenses involved in doing so. He is also involving his whole family in the fraud."

If the same homeowner is convinced that his or her *taxes are unfairly higher than those of his neighbors,* he was repeatedly advised to go fight City Hall rather than try to conceal his new wing:

"There are proper channels through which grievances can be submitted. To make one's own judgment would be wrong. One should abide by the rules of the community and its decisions. If there is wrongdoing in the office of the tax assessor, then it would be one's duty to correct things at that level."

"He should investigate his suspicions on tax rates and values. If his taxes are incorrect, there are proper channels to correct the error. His cheating still would not be justified."

Or in the words of one homeowner: "Grin and bear it—Fight and grow weary."

Suppose a handyman says that if you pay in cash, he will not charge sales tax.

Once again, the argument was raised that the practice is

common, along with the comment, "I don't know of anyone who wouldn't agree 90 percent of the time."

Those who called it wrong added such comments as: "The handyman has a commitment to the state and is withholding what does not belong to him." . . . "He is robbing the government." . . . "The fee should be the same whether it is paid in cash or not. By this statement, the handyman sounds like a rip-off artist."

Those who refused to call this practice wrong left the matter in the hands of the handyman: "I always pay in cash. It's up to him what he does." . . . "What he does with the money is his own business. I paid what he asked for." . . . "This is a form of his salesmanship. Who can say he is wrong? He might make up the sales tax for the government himself."

When moral theologians discussed taxation, they offered cold comfort to tax evaders. They were on the side of the Internal Revenue Service. Father Curran cited a "moral obligation to pay just taxes" and "the presumption is that they are just." In agreeing on the obligation to pay taxes, Professor Milhaven added that "if others are tax scoundrels that is no reason to evade taxes." He noted that "so many people need government assistance"—which is financed by taxes. Those "who are ripping off are doing something to themselves," what he called "intrinsic punishment" that is self-inflicted because of what deception and evasion of responsibility do to their human dignity.

By inventing deductions, taxpayers are "shirking their responsibility," Father Kenny said, and added that if the government is taxing unfairly and wasting tax monies, then the appropriate response is to work for reform, not evade taxes. To Father McCormick, faking deductions is lying and out of order on the face of it. Dr. Shinn's comments followed a similar line: "A person assumes a big burden of proof in being deliberately dishonest—it takes an extreme case to justify it."

"By and large," Dr. Farley said, "honesty is called for in relating to the tax system." If you think the system of taxation is justified on the whole "as a way of redistributing resources in a society" (and she does), you have the responsibility of being "faithful to the system." As for taking personal exceptions and using personal evasions, you would have "to be placed in really dire straits where your

85

basic needs were not being met—in which case it really would be unjust to you." However, since no tax system is going to be "totally fair in every single regard, for the sake of affirming the system, one does accept some unfairness." On the other hand, civil disobedience regarding some forms of taxation (e.g., refusing to pay a specific form of federal tax because it is earmarked for weapons in what one judges to be an evil war) may be justified.

After Father McNulty pointed out that an arrangement to evade the sales tax involved dishonesty and that normal channels of protest should be used to protest real estate taxes, he set before taxpayers the "responsible" question to ask and to answer personally and individually:

"Do you feel in conscience that you are making an honest effort to pay sensible taxes?

"The people devising the whole tax system know that they can't possibly cover every single detail and case so they allow for responsible leeway. The taxpayer has to walk a narrow line between rationalizing evasion and exercising responsible leeway."

10
The Bottom Line

> *"Each specific case must be decided on its own merits and very often we won't be certain even then." (Protestant theologian)*

> *"Yes, individual acts and cases are important. We do have to get down to the bottom line of doing right or wrong." (Catholic theologian)*

Moral theologians deserve only the next-to-last word.

The last word belongs to each individual.

These closing words will be distilled—without direct quotations—from the dialogues with moral theologians and from the statements of individual Christians. They spin a web of Monday morality around the twofold Commandment of Love and the Golden Rule.

In everyday morality, theologians are more useful for the leading questions they can ask than for the ready answers they can't give.

In everyday morality, integrity is what you tend to expect of others first, yourself second, instead of the way it should be—the other way around.

Out there where individual Christians conduct their lives, original sin, evil, human frailty exist. No wishful idealism will erase that reality and the unavoidable consequence: compromise in everyday morality.

A rough kind of justice emerges. Christians may end up with moral decisions that are less than ideal. Deprived of reassuring clear-cut, either-or choices, they juggle, they balance, they compromise.

Compromise can comfort or discomfort. For some, it's an easy, self-serving way out; for others, it's an unavoidable choice between two undesirables.

With compromise comes the risk of rationalization, such as the following Ten "Commandments" of Rationalization encountered in everyday morality:

1. *Caveat Emptor.*
2. *I'm only getting even.*
3. *Everyone's doing it.*
4. *It doesn't hurt anyone.*
5. *It's just a drop in the bucket (when big government and large institutions are involved).*
6. *Only doing what I'm expected to do.*
7. *They would only do the same to me.*
8. *Those on top do it.*
9. *It's my own business what I do.*
10. *I'll make up for it.*

In everyday morality, ask, instead: Would you approve of the other person acting that way toward you?

Besides the other person, there is that amorphous, vague floating presence of evil in the world. Do you want to add to it?

What about the *system* in which you live? Where do you draw the line between the moral and the legal? They are not always the same. The legal is defined by the established and by the establishment.

Defying the legal order for purely personal gain is different from defying it for a larger goal of helping others and transforming society. Conscientious objection comes from the conscience, not from conscious pursuit of advantage.

The community-at-large figures in. Conscientious moral decisions can't be completely self-centered or self-inflicted. The way others view similar situations deserves a second look, particularly those sensitive others respected for the lives they lead.

Compromise in everyday morality can be like shaking a tree. Ask: Why is it shaken? For conscientious and unselfish reasons? Or for personal gain and advantage? As a balancing of responsibilities? For proportionate reasons?

What falls to the ground?

Is convention dictating a decision to shake or not to shake? Then it would be a matter of accepting the accepted because it's accepted. Morality would become a matter of convention over conscience.

Finally, who is this person that is choosing? What kind of moral life is being created by choices? What kind of person is being created by the moral choices?

Since no one is usually watching in the realm of Monday morality, the matter is private. No one may be aware of choices made, temptations resisted, sacrifices made. No other human being may know—or care. Except you, the last word.